CW00487251

SALTER AIR FRYER COOKBOOK

FOR BEGINNERS 2023

1001-Day Healthy and Easy Salter Air Fryer Recipes for Smart People

CONTENTS

DESSERTS RECIPES 65

POULTRY RECIPES 78

FISH & SEAFOOD RECIPES...90

SANDWICHES & BURGERS RECIPES 104

INTRODUCTION

Air fryers are full of hot air, and that's what is great about them. They are basically small, powerful ovens, and ovens use air as a vehicle for heat, whereas deep frying uses fat as the vehicle for heat. Because air fryers are ovens and not fryers, foods that come out of your air fryer will not be 100% identical to the onion rings at Cone-n-Shake or the calamari rings at your favorite bar and grill. The upshot is that air fryers are much less messy and oil-intensive than deep-frying. Even better, these lil' ovens can do much more than crank out faux fried food. Air fryers bring beautifully browned vegetables, crackly-skinned chicken wings, and even light and airy cakes, all within your reach.

HOW AIR FRYERS WORK

Your air fryer is like an amazing convection oven. It's small, yet mighty, and you can roast, broil, or bake in it. You cannot deep fry in it. Need a refresher on convection cooking? No problem.

Heat rises, so in a regular oven the top rack is always the hottest spot, which leads to uneven doneness. (It's also why a lot of cookie recipes tell you to rotate baking sheets from top to bottom and back to front midway through baking.) In a convection oven, however, fans blow hot air around so the temperature is equalized throughout the oven.Air fryers aren't *exactly* like convection ovens; their airflow is designed to more closely replicate the heat distribution of deep-frying in hot fat. But for our purposes, the convection oven analogy is good enough.

IMPORTANT TIPS TO KEEP IN MIND

1. Always have the grate in the basket. This allows hot air to circulate around the food, and also keeps the food from sitting in excess oil.
2. Air fryers are loud. When it's running, you'll hear whirring fans.
3. It's hands-on. Even browning requires you to remove the basket and shuffle the food around every few minutes.
4. It's fine to pull out the basket for a peek. You can do this at any point into the cooking process. No need to shut off the machine, as it shuts itself off when the basket is out.
5. Accordingly, make sure the drawer is pushed all the way in, or it won't turn back on. You'll know, because the air fryer will be suddenly quiet.
6. Food cooks fast, faster than you're used to! It's one of the best attributes of the air fryer. Your air fryer's manual likely has a handy table of cooking times and temperatures for common foods. The less food in the basket, the shorter the cook time will be; the more food, the longer it will be.
7. You may need a slightly lower temperature. A lot of air fryer recipes call for lower temperature settings than their conventional counterparts. This might seem fishy, but just go with it. Once again, air fryers get hot very fast and move that hot air around, so a slightly lower temperature will help keep food from getting too dark or crispy on the outside, while still being properly cooked on the inside.

MISTAKES TO AVOID

1. **Don't be too generous with oil.** Use a light hand with that oil! Excess oil ends up in the drawer under the grate, but if there's too much buildup, it might smoke. Generally speaking, if there's already fat on the food (skin-on chicken, for example, or frozen fried food), you might not need to oil the food at all. Vegetables, however, benefit from a light coating of oil, because it helps make them nice and brown.

2. **Don't grease the drawer with cooking spray.** Seems like that would be a good idea, right? But the baskets have nonstick coating, and cooking spray can damage the finish over time. (Really, it says so in the manual! What, didn't you read it?) In lieu of cooking spray, toss your food in oil instead—you're probably doing that already, in many cases—or rub it down with an oil-saturated paper towel. I found pre-fried frozen foods didn't need the help of extra grease.

3. **Don't crowd the drawer.** It's so tempting to add another handful of potato sticks or shaved beets, but you'll learn from experience that food comes out crisper and cooks up faster if you work in small batches.

4. **Don't neglect to shake the basket.** Doing this periodically ensures food is evenly exposed to heat, which gives you better browning. A lot of recipes call for you to shake the basket every five minutes. For larger items, like breaded fish fillets, flip them instead. If a recipe calls for shaking or flipping and you skip it, it's not detrimental, but it'll keep you from achieving that lucrative, oh-so-similar-to-fried-food result.

5. **Don't just dump the hot contents of the drawer into a bowl.** Use tongs or a spoon to get cooked food out. Excess oil collects under the removable grate in your basket, so if you yank out the basket and tip it onto a platter, the oil will come spilling out along with the grate. This can burn you, make a mess, and lead to greasy food.

6. **Don't trust the timer 100%.** A lot of basket-style air fryers have a dial you set like an old-fashioned kitchen timer, or like that kid's game Perfection. When the time's up it goes PING! and the machine stops. On one of the models I used, five minutes flew by suspiciously fast. So I set my phone's timer when I set the air fryer's timer, and guess what—the appliance was off by a few minutes. This is not a big deal; with air fryers, you just keep re-setting the timer until the food is done to your liking. But do realize that not all timers run accurately.

7. **Don't put the hot drawer on the countertop.** Think of the drawer as a hot pan. When you pull it from the unit, the bottom especially will be hot. Grab the drawer by the handle, not the other parts, and have a trivet or potholder ready to set it on if heat will damage your countertop.

8. **Don't get all touchy-feely with the air fryer.** The exterior of the air fryer can get hot (the back, likely). Not hot enough to burn you, but don't get all grabby with it.

HOW TO CLEAN YOUR AIR FRYER

It's important to clean your air fryer after every use, since a build-up of oil can make the unit smoke. In some instances, you can simply wipe off the drawer and grate with a paper towel. If they're gunky, hand wash. Most models have parts that are dishwasher safe, so check with your manual.

SALADS & SIDE DISHES RECIPES

Pita Chips & Hummus

Servings: 4
Cooking Time: 9 Minutes

Ingredients:

- 5 thin pitas
- Spray oil
- Hummus
- 1 can garbanzo beans (15.5 ounces), drained and rinsed
- 1 tablespoon tahini
- 2 garlic cloves, grated
- 3 tablespoons olive oil
- 1 lemon, juiced
- Salt, to taste
- Items Needed
- Food proccessor or blender

Directions:

1. Select the Preheat function on the Air Fryer, adjust the temperature to 370°F, then press Start/Pause.
2. Cut the pitas in half, then cut each half into 4 equal triangles.
3. Place the pita pieces into the preheated air fryer and spray them with oil until they are evenly coated on all sides.
4. Set the temperature to 370°F, time to 9 minutes, then press Start/Pause
5. Shake the basket halfway through the cooking time.
6. Remove the pita chips when done. Let them sit in a bowl for 10 minutes before serving – they will continue to crisp as they cool down.
7. Place the garbanzo beans in a food processor or blender along with the tahini and garlic. Blend until smooth, then add in the olive oil with the motor running. Thin out by blending in with a tablespoon or so of water as needed, if the texture seems too thick. Season the hummus to taste with lemon juice and salt, then serve with the pita chips.

Air Fryer Sauteed Onions

Servings: 2
Cooking Time: 13 Minutes

Ingredients:

- 1 onion
- 1 tablespoon oil
- a small pinch of sugar

Directions:

1. Cut onion into long slices.
2. Heal oil in an air fryer pan on 300 degrees for 1 minute.
3. Place onion slices in the pan and mix evenly to coat the onion with oil.
4. Cook onions on 300 degrees for 5 minutes, stirring halfway through.
5. Add a small pinch of sugar to onions, mix thoroughly, and cook for another 7-10 minutes stirring event 2-3 minutes.
6. Remove pan from air fryer and enjoy with your favorite recipe immediately!

Air Fryer Falafel Salad

Servings: 4

Ingredients:

- 2 cloves garlic
- 4 scallions, whites and greens, thinly sliced, separated
- 6 1/2 c. baby kale, divided
- 2 15-ounce cans chickpeas, drained and rinsed
- 1 tsp. grated lemon zest
- 2 tbsp. all-purpose flour
- 1 tsp. ground cumin
- 1 tsp. ground coriander
- Kosher salt
- 2 tbsp. lemon juice
- 3 tbsp. olive oil, divided, plus more for basket
- 1/2 English cucumber, thinly sliced on bias
- 1/2 c. fresh parsley leaves
- 1/4 c. fresh mint leaves
- Greek yogurt, for topping

Directions:

1. In food processor, pulse garlic, scallion whites, and 1/2 cup baby kale until very finely chopped. Add chickpeas, lemon zest, flour, cumin, coriander, and 1/2 tsp salt and pulse to combine (chickpeas should be chopped but coarse). Form mixture into twenty-four 2-tablespoon balls.
2. Heat air fryer to 325°F. Brush insert of basket with oil and add 12 falafel. Air-fry 15 minutes. Brush falafel with 1 tablespoon oil and increase air fryer temperature to 400°F. Air-fry until deeply golden, 4 more minutes. Repeat with remaining falafel.
3. In large bowl, whisk together lemon juice and remaining 2 tablespoons olive oil. Add cucumbers and marinate, 5 minutes. Add remaining 6 cups baby kale, parsley, and mint leaves, scallion greens, and 1/2 tsp salt and toss. Top with falafel and dollop of yogurt.

Tuna Egg Salad

Servings: 1
Cooking Time: 15 Minutes

Ingredients:
- 2 hard boiled eggs
- 1 2.6 oz packet light tuna in water (I use less sodium)
- 1 tablespoon mayonnaise ((check labels for whole30))
- 2 tablespoons chopped red onion
- salt and pepper (to taste)

Directions:
1. Chop the eggs and add them to a bowl with the tuna, mayo and red onion.
2. Mix to combine and season with salt and pepper to taste.
3. Eat right out of the bowl with a spoon or piled on a piece of toast, in a wrap, over greens, etc.

Air Fryer Green Bean Casserole

Servings: 6
Cooking Time: 12 Minutes

Ingredients:
- 10.5 ounce Cream of Mushroom Soup
- 1/2 cup milk
- 4 cups cooked cut green beans
- 1/2 tsp salt
- 1/2 tsp black pepper
- 1 1/2 cups crispy fried onions

Directions:
1. In a medium bowl, combine the soup, milk, salt, and pepper.
2. Stir in the green beans and half of the fried onions.
3. Pour mixture into the baking dish and cook for 350 degrees F for 12 minutes, stirring halfway through the cooking time.
4. Once done, top the baking dish with the remaining fried onions, and cook for an additional 2-3 minutes.

Crispy Smashed Potatoes With Herb Aioli

Servings: 2-4

Ingredients:
- Herb Aioli:
- ½ cup light mayo
- 1 teaspoon light sour cream
- 1 tablespoon fresh parsley, chopped
- 1 tablespoon fresh basil, chiffonade
- 1 tablespoon fresh chives, chopped
- 1 tablespoon fresh dill, chopped
- 1 tablespoon lemon juice
- ¼ teaspoon lemon zest
- 2 teaspoons extra virgin olive oil
- Kosher salt and pepper, to taste
- Potatoes:
- 1½ pounds small creamer potatoes
- 3 tablespoons avocado oil
- ¼ teaspoon cayenne pepper
- ½ teaspoon garlic powder
- 1 tablespoon black pepper

- 2 teaspoons kosher salt, plus more for boiling water
- ¼ teaspoon smoked paprika (optional)
- Oil spray

Directions:
1. Mix all the ingredients for the herb aioli in a small bowl and set aside to chill in the refrigerator.
2. Place the potatoes in a medium pot filled with cold salted water.
3. Boil the potatoes until a knife easily pierces through without any resistance.
4. Strain the potatoes and let cool for easy handling.
5. Combine the potatoes, avocado oil, cayenne pepper, garlic powder, black pepper, salt, and smoked paprika in a small bowl. Toss to coat.
6. Smash the potatoes gently with the palm of your hands, crushing them only halfway so that they stay intact.
7. Coat the Smart Air Fryer basket lightly with oil spray.
8. Place the potatoes directly into the air fryer basket, without the crisper plate.
9. Select the Air Fry function, adjust temperature to 400°F and time to 15 minutes, then press Start/Pause.
10. Remove the potatoes when done.
11. Serve hot with a side of aioli.

Spicy Canned Salmon Salad Rice Bowl

Servings: 1
Cooking Time: 0 Minutes

Ingredients:
- 1 5-ounce can skinless wild pink or red salmon (in water drained)
- 1 tablespoons light mayonnaise
- 2 teaspoons sriracha sauce (plus more for topping)
- 2 scallions (white and greens separated)
- Pinch kosher salt
- 3/4 cup cooked brown rice (heated)

- ½ cup chopped cucumber (I use Persian cucumbers)
- Furikake or chopped nori and sesame seeds (for garnish)

Directions:
1. In a small bowl, combine the salmon, mayonnaise, sriracha, scallion whites and pinch of salt and mix well.
2. In the bowl you plan to serve in, add the rice.
3. Top it with the salmon salad, chopped cucumber, furikake and scallion greens plus more sriracha if desired.

Chicken Caprese Salad Recipe

Servings: 4
Cooking Time: 10 Minutes

Ingredients:
- FOR THE CHICKEN:
- 2 tbsp Balsamic vinegar
- 1 tbsp Olive oil
- 1/2 tsp Garlic powder
- 1 tsp Dried basil
- 1/2 tsp Dried oregano
- 1 tsp Sea salt
- 1/4 tsp Black pepper
- 4 8-oz Boneless skinless chicken breasts
- FOR THE SALAD:
- 5 cups Romaine lettuce (chopped)
- 1 cup Cherry tomatoes (halved)
- 1/2 cup Fresh mozzarella balls
- 1/4 cup Fresh basil (cut into ribbons)
- 1/4 cup Balsamic glaze

Directions:
1. In a large bowl, whisk together balsamic vinegar, olive oil, garlic powder, dried basil, dried oregano, sea salt, and black pepper. Add the chicken breasts and turn to coat in the marinade. Set aside to marinate for at least 10 minutes, or marinate in the fridge for up to 8 hours.
2. Cook chicken breasts in the air fryer like this or in the oven like this. (Use the ingredients above, and check these links for cook times

and temperatures based on your preferred method.)

3. Let the chicken rest for 5 minutes, then slice against the grain. Cover to keep warm.
4. Meanwhile, make the balsamic glaze like this.
5. In a large salad bowl, combine lettuce, tomatoes, mozzarella balls, and chicken.
6. Sprinkle the salad with basil leaves and drizzle with balsamic glaze.

Air Fryer Bacon-wrapped Stuffed Jalapenos

Servings: 6
Cooking Time: 14 Minutes

Ingredients:
- 12 Jalapenos
- 8 ounces of cream cheese, room temperature or slightly soft
- 1/2 cup shredded cheddar cheese
- 1/4 teaspoon garlic powder
- 1/8 teaspoon onion powder
- 12 slices of bacon, thinly cut
- salt and pepper to taste

Directions:
1. Cut the jalapenos in half, remove the stems, and remove the seeds and membranes. The more membrane you leave, the spicier the jalapenos will be.
2. Add cream cheese, shredded cheddar cheese, garlic powder, onion powder, salt, and pepper in a bowl. Mix to combine.
3. Using a small spoon, scoop the cream mixture into each jalapeno filling it just to the top.
4. Preheat air fryer to 350 degrees for about 3 minutes.
5. Cut each slice of bacon in half.
6. Wrap each jalapeno half in one piece of bacon.
7. Place the bacon-wrapped stuffed jalapenos in the air fryer in an even layer making sure they do not touch.

8. Air fry at 350 degrees for 14-16 minutes, until bacon is thoroughly cooked.
9. Enjoy immediately or refrigerate for up to 3 days, reheating before eating.

Grilled Peach & Burrata Salad

Servings: 4

Ingredients:
- 2 peaches, cut into ½-inch-thick wedges
- 4 tablespoons olive oil, divided
- Kosher salt, to taste
- 6 cups arugula
- 8 ounces burrata cheese, torn
- ¼ cup toasted hazelnuts, chopped
- ¼ cup fresh mint leaves, torn
- 2 tablespoons balsamic vinegar, for drizzling
- Flaky sea salt, for finishing
- Freshly ground black pepper, for finishing

Directions:
1. Place the crisper plate into the Smart Air Fryer basket.
2. Select the Preheat function, then press Start/Pause.
3. Place the peaches and 1½ tablespoons olive oil in a medium bowl and toss to coat. Season with salt to taste.
4. Place the peaches onto the preheated crisper plate.
5. Select the Veggies function, adjust time to 9 minutes, then press Start/Pause.
6. Shake the peaches halfway through cooking. The Shake Reminder will let you know when.
7. Remove the peaches when done.
8. Divide the arugula between 4 plates and top with equal portions of peaches, burrata cheese, hazelnuts, and mint.
9. Drizzle the remaining olive oil and balsamic vinegar over each salad, season with flaky sea salt and freshly ground black pepper, then serve.

BEEF, PORK & LAMB RECIPES

Air Fryer Breaded Cubed Steak

Servings: 4
Cooking Time: 20 Minutes

Ingredients:
- 4 pieces cubed steak (beef round sirloin) (16 ounces total)
- 3 large eggs (with 1 tablespoon water)
- 1 1/4 teaspoons salt
- 1 cup seasoned breadcrumbs*
- olive oil spray
- white rice and lime wedges (optional for serving)

Directions:
1. Season the beef with salt on both sides.
2. Beat the eggs in a shallow bowl with water.
3. Dip the beef in the egg, then into the breadcrumbs, patting it with the back of a fork so it sticks.
4. Transfer to the air fryer basket in batches as needed.
5. Spray the top of the beef with oil then air fry 400F in a single layer 5 minutes on each side, spraying the other side when you flip. Serve with rice and lime wedges, if desired.

Air Fryer Mexican Pizza

Servings: 2
Cooking Time: 10 Minutes

Ingredients:
- ½ lb ground beef
- 1 tbsp taco seasoning
- 4 flour tortillas
- 1 tsp oil
- 4 tbsp refried beans
- ½ cup salsa
- 1 cup red enchilada sauce
- 1½ cups sharp cheddar jack cheese shredded
- 2 tbsp black olives
- 1 Roma tomato diced
- optional toppings shredded lettuce, green onions, sour cream

Directions:
1. In a small skillet, brown the ground beef until no longer pink. Stir in the taco seasoning until combined, and remove from heat.
2. Use a small skillet and heat the skillet over medium-high heat. Lightly brown the tortillas about 1 minute per side, or until lightly browned and slightly crispy. Set aside. (You can also heat the tortillas in the air fryer. Add the tortillas to the basket of the air fryer and then add a trivet to the top to keep them from flying around. Heat the air fryer to 370 degrees Fahrenheit and air fryer for 3 minutes. Carefully remove the trivet, it will be hot)
3. Place a tortilla into the basket of the air fryer. Spread the top of the tortilla with refried beans. Top the beans with taco meat and with salsa.
4. Add the second tortilla on top of the first. Cover the top of the tortilla with enchilada sauce, diced tomatoes, shredded cheese, green onions, and black olives. Then top with additional shredded cheese.
5. Air fry the Mexican pizza at 370 degrees Fahrenheit for 2-3 minutes. Use a spatula to carefully remove the pizza from the air fryer to a serving plate. Top with lettuce, sour cream, and green onion tops before serving. Repeat the process for the second pizza.

NOTES

I make this recipe in my Cosori 5.8 qt. air fryer or 6.8 quart air fryer. Depending on your air fryer, size and wattages, cooking time may need to be adjusted 1-2 minutes.

If you want to have crispy tortillas for this recipe, you must stick to flour. This copycat version relies on the crispiness of the tortillas to hold sturdy for all those toppings!

Air-fryer Pork Chops

Servings: 4
Cooking Time: 15 Minutes

Ingredients:
- 1/3 cup almond flour
- 1/4 cup grated Parmesan cheese
- 1 teaspoon garlic powder
- 1 teaspoon Creole seasoning
- 1 teaspoon paprika
- 4 boneless pork loin chops (6 ounces each)
- Cooking spray

Directions:
1. Preheat air fryer to 375F. In a shallow bowl, combine almond flour, cheese, garlic powder, Creole seasoning and paprika. Coat pork chops with flour mixture; shake off excess. Working in batches as needed, place chops in single layer on greased tray in air-fryer basket; spritz with cooking spray.
2. Cook until golden brown, 12-15 minutes or until a thermometer reads 145F, turning halfway through cooking and spritzing with additional cooking spray. Remove and keep warm. Repeat with remaining chops.

Air Fryer Bacon Recipe

Servings: 8
Cooking Time: 7 Minutes

Ingredients:
- 8 slices Bacon
- 1/2 cup Water (optional)

Directions:
1. Preheat the air fryer to 370 degrees F (187 degrees C).
2. Optional step: Add a little bit of water to the air fryer drip tray, to prevent smoking. Use just enough to cover the bottom of the tray below the grate; this was 1/2 cup in my air fryer.
3. Arrange the bacon in a single layer in the air fryer rack or basket, overlapping slightly. (Bacon in the air fryer will shrink as it cooks.) Depending on the size and shape of your air fryer, it may help to cut the bacon pieces in half.
4. Cook for 6 minutes. Open the air fryer and spread out the bacon pieces so that they aren't overlapping. Cook for 1-4 more minutes for regular bacon, or 3-5 more minutes for thick cut bacon, or until done to your liking.

Air Fryer Full English

Servings: 4
Cooking Time: 20 Minutes

Ingredients:
- 8 bacon medallions
- 4 reduced fat pork sausages
- 4 medium eggs beaten
- 420 g tin of baked beans
- 200 g cherry tomatoes
- 200 g button mushrooms
- low calorie cooking spray
- salt and pepper to taste

Directions:
1. Pre-heat your air fryer to 180°C.
2. Take a sheet of foil and place the mushrooms onto it. Spray with low calorie cooking spray and season with salt and pepper. Scrunch the edges together to seal it into a pouch. It should look like a pasty that has been stood up.
3. Take a sheet of foil and place the tomatoes onto it. Spray with low calorie cooking spray and season with salt and pepper. Scrunch it into a pouch.
4. Place the sausages and foil pouches into the air fryer for 5 minutes.
5. After 5 minutes, add the bacon medallions. You will need to overlap them to fit in most air fryers - this is fine!
6. After another 5 minutes, open the air fryer and push the bacon into a pile to make room. Add two small ovenproof bowls, one with the baked beans and one with the

beaten eggs. Close the air fryer and cook for another 5 minutes.

7. Open the air fryer again and mix the eggs with a fork, close the lid and cook for a further 2 minutes.

8. Turn off the air fryer and mix up the eggs. Plate up the breakfasts and serve!

Spicy Air Fryer Pork Belly With Kabocha Squash

Servings: 2

Ingredients:
- Deselect All
- Gochujang Sauce:
- 2 tablespoons gochujang (Korean red chile paste)
- 1 tablespoon toasted sesame oil
- 1 teaspoon mirin
- 1 teaspoon soy sauce
- 1 teaspoon sugar
- 1 clove garlic, finely grated
- Pork Belly and Squash:
- 1/2 kabocha squash (about 1 1/4 pounds), seeds removed and quartered into wedges
- Nonstick cooking spray
- Kosher salt and freshly ground black pepper
- 1 piece skinless pork belly (about 1 pound)
- 1 scallion, thinly sliced on bias
- Toasted sesame seeds, for sprinkling
- Cooked white rice, for serving

Directions:
1. Special equipment: a 6-quart air fryer
2. Preheat a 6-quart air fryer to 375 degrees F.
3. For the gochujang sauce: Stir together the jarred gochujang, sesame oil, mirin, soy sauce, sugar and garlic in a small bowl; set aside.
4. For the pork belly and squash: Spray the kabocha squash with cooking spray and season with 1/4 teaspoon salt. Set aside.
5. Season the pork belly with 1/2 teaspoon salt and pepper. Place the pork belly in the basket of a 6-quart air fryer, then spray it lightly with cooking spray. Air fry until the pork belly browns and crisps on top and around the edges, about 25 minutes. Flip the pork belly over with cooking tongs and then arrange the kabocha squash around the perimeter. Cook until the pork belly is crisp all over and the squash is tender and charred, about 20 minutes. Brush the pork belly with the gochujang sauce, letting any excess run off. Cook until the sauce is slightly sticky and charred, 3 to 4 minutes more.

6. Remove the pork belly onto a plate and let rest for 10 minutes (the squash can keep warm in the air fryer). Cut into 1/4- to 1/2-inch-thick slices and brush with more sauce, if desired. Sprinkle the scallion and sesame seeds over the pork belly and serve with the squash, rice and remaining sauce.

Air-fryer Beef Wellington Wontons

Servings: 3-1/2
Cooking Time: 10 Minutes

Ingredients:
- 1/2 pound lean ground beef (90% lean)
- 1 tablespoon butter
- 1 tablespoon olive oil
- 2 garlic cloves, minced
- 1-1/2 teaspoons chopped shallot
- 1 cup each chopped fresh shiitake, baby portobello and white mushrooms
- 1/4 cup dry red wine
- 1 tablespoon minced fresh parsley
- 1/2 teaspoon salt
- 1/4 teaspoon pepper
- 1 package (12 ounces) wonton wrappers
- 1 large egg
- 1 tablespoon water
- Cooking spray

Directions:
1. Preheat air fryer to 325F. In a small skillet, cook and crumble beef over medium heat until no longer pink, 4-5 minutes. Transfer to a large bowl. In the same skillet, heat butter and olive oil over medium-high heat. Add garlic and shallot; cook 1 minute. Stir

in mushrooms and wine. Cook until mushrooms are tender, 8-10 minutes; add to beef. Stir in parsley, salt and pepper.

2. Place about 2 teaspoons filling in the center of each wonton wrapper. Combine egg and water. Moisten wonton edges with egg mixture; fold opposite corners over filling and press to seal.

3. In batches, arrange wontons in a single layer on greased tray in air-fryer basket; spritz with cooking spray. Cook until lightly browned, 4-5 minutes. Turn; spritz with cooking spray. Cook until golden brown and crisp, 4-5 minutes longer. Serve warm.

Air Fryer Ribs Recipe
Servings: 4
Cooking Time: 28 Minutes

Ingredients:
- Ribs and Dry Rub:
- 3 pounds baby back pork ribs (1 rack)
- 3 teaspoons garlic powder
- 2 teaspoons paprika
- 1 teaspoon salt
- 1/2 teaspoon black pepper
- 1/2 teaspoon cumin
- Sweet and Sticky BBQ Sauce
- 1/2 cup ketchup
- 2 tablespoons brown sugar
- 1 tablespoon apple cider vinegar
- 1 tablespoon olive oil
- 1/2 teaspoon ground cumin
- salt and pepper to taste

Directions:
1. Remove the membrane: Peel off the silverskin from the back of the ribs.
2. Cut the rack of pork ribs into 2-3 sections so that it can fit into your air fryer basket.
3. Make the spice rub: In a small bowl, mix garlic powder, paprika, salt, pepper and cumin.
4. Season the baby back ribs: Pat the ribs dry and rub the ribs on all sides with the spice rub.

5. Cook the ribs in the air fryer: Preheat the air fryer to 375F/190C for a few minutes. Once hot, place the ribs into the basket with the meat side down and cook for 15 minutes.

   (It's important to let the air fryer to heat up first to avoid the ribs from sticking to the basket.)
6. Flip the ribs using kitchen tongs, and cook for 10 more minutes at 375F/190C.
7. Make the BBQ sauce: While the ribs are cooking, you can add bbq sauce ingredients in a saucepan. Heat over medium-low heat until the sugar and salt are completely dissolved.
8. Brush with BBQ sauce: Remove the basket from the air fryer and brush generously with barbecue sauce on all sides.
9. Place the basket back in the air fryer and cook for 3-5 more minutes at 400F/200C, or until the sauce has set and darkened slightly. (It may take more or less time based on the thickness or your ribs)
10. Remove the ribs from the basket and let them rest for 5 minutes so that the juices can redistribute through the meat. Feel free to brush with more barbeque sauce if you like.

Notes
You can also use spare ribs for this recipe, but make sure to cook for a longer time as spare ribs are usually larger.

If you'd like to make this recipe low carb and keto friend, you can use low carb sugar.
Check frequently during the last few minutes so that your ribs won't get burned.

Thick Pork Chops In The Air Fryer
Servings: 4
Cooking Time: 25 Minutes
Ingredients:
- 2 teaspoon chili powder
- 1 teaspoon garlic powder
- ½ teaspoon salt

- ½ teaspoon sugar
- 1 lime zested
- 4 thick-cut pork chops
- Cilantro, optional
- Lime wedges, optional

Directions:
1. Preheat your air fryer to 400 degrees F.
2. Combine the chili powder, garlic powder, salt, sugar, and lime zest in a bowl.* Spray your pork chops with olive oil cooking spray and then cover each pork chop completely with the seasoning.
3. Play them into the air fryer with a little space around them and cook for 20 to 25 minutes. You may need to cook in batches. If you have varying thicknesses in your pork chops, then use a meat thermometer on your smallest pork chop and set it at 145 degrees F.
4. Allow pork chops to cool for 5 minutes before slicing.
5. Enjoy!

NOTES
*You can also use 1 ½ tablespoon store-bought chili lime seasoning instead of homemade seasoning. I use Trader Joe's chile lime seasoning.

HOW TO REHEAT THICK CUT PORK CHOPS IN THE AIR FRYER
Preheat the air fryer to 350 degrees F.
Lay the leftover chops in a single layer.
Cook for 4 to 6 minutes until heated through.

Prunes In Bacon

Servings: 10

Ingredients:
- 500g pitted prunes (45 pieces)
- 23 slices bacon (3 mm thick)

Directions:
1. Cut the slices of bacon in half and wrap each prune with the cut slice. Pierce with a toothpick to hold together.
2. Insert crisper paniere in pan and pan in unit. Select AIR FRY, set temperature to 200°C, and set time to 13 minutes. Press START/STOP to begin and allow to preheat for 3 minutes.
3. After the unit has preheated, place the prunes with bacon on the crisper paniere in the pan and reinsert the pan into the main unit.
4. Remove pan from unit after 2 minutes and shake prunes or toss them with silicone-tipped tongs. Reinsert pan to resume cooking.
5. After 8 minutes, place the prunes on a serving dish to enjoy right away.
6. TIP You can soak the prunes for 30 minutes in cider before wrapping them with the bacon for added flavour.

Air Fryer Ham And Cheese Melt

Servings: 1
Cooking Time: 10 Minutes

Ingredients:
- 2 slices bread
- 2-4 slices good melting cheese (American, Swiss, cheddar, Gruyere, etc.)
- 1-2 slices ham , about 1/4-inch thick
- 1 Tablespoon (15 g) butter

Directions:
1. Layer the bread, cheese, ham, another slice of cheese, and then the top slice of bread (you want the ham in-between the cheese so when it melts, the cheese will hold everything together).
2. Butter the outsides of bread. Make sure to butter both the top and bottom slice.
3. Secure the top slice of bread with toothpicks through the sandwich. Lay sandwich in air fryer basket.
4. Air Fry at 360°F/182°C for about 3-5 minutes to melt the cheese.
5. Flip the sandwich and increase heat to 380°F/193°C to finish and crisp the bread. Air Fry at 380°F/193°C for about 5 minutes or until the sandwich is to your preferred texture. Check on the sandwich often to make sure it doesn't burn (different breads

will toast quicker or slower than others). Allow to cool a bit before biting into the yummy grilled cheese sandwich!

NOTES

If your bread is really thin, it will blow off in the air fryer because of the hot circulating air. Use toothpicks to secure the sandwich during air frying. Remember to remove the toothpicks before eating.

Air Fryer Sliders

Servings: 6-8
Cooking Time: 10 Minutes

Ingredients:

- 1 lb. (454 g) ground beef (or chicken, turkey, pork, lamb)
- 1 Tablespoon (30 ml) Worcestershire sauce
- 1/2 teaspoon (2.5 ml) garlic powder
- salt , to taste
- black pepper , to taste
- 6-8 slider buns or rolls
- BURGER TOPPINGS:
- lettuce, tomato, pickles, onion slices, blue cheese, avocado, bacon, fried onions, etc.
- ketchup, mustard, mayo, gochujang, hot sauce, bbq sauce, etc.

Directions:

1. Preheat the air fryer at 380°F/193°C for 5 minutes.
2. Mix together the beef, Worcestershire, and garlic powder until just combined. Divide mixture into 6-8 even balls. Lightly flatten each ball to form a small patty. For best texture, try not to overwork the patties. Form them just enough so that the patties hold their shape.
3. Lightly spray patties with oil. Season liberal amount of salt and pepper on top of patties.
4. Spray the air fryer basket/tray with oil & place the sliders in the basket/tray.
5. Air fry 380°F/193°C for 5 minutes. Flip the patties and cook for another 1-3 minutes, or until the center is cooked to your preferred doneness or internal temperature reaches 160°F.

6. For Cheeseburger Sliders: add the slices of cheese on top of the cooked patties. Air fry at 380°F/193°C for about 30 seconds to 1 minute to melt the cheese.
7. For best juiciness, cover the patties and let rest for a couple minutes. While patties are resting, warm the buns in the air fryer at 380°F/193°C for about 1 minute. Serve on buns, topped with your favorite toppings.

Air Fryer Beef Jerky

Ingredients:

- 2 pounds flank steak
- 1/2 cup low-sodium soy sauce
- 2 tablespoons Worcestershire sauce
- 2 teaspoons coarsely-ground black pepper
- 1 teaspoon liquid smoke
- 1 teaspoon onion powder
- 1 teaspoon seasoned salt
- 1/2 teaspoon garlic powder

Directions:

1. Thinly slice the steak into 1/8-inch thick strips, either with the grain (which will result in a chewier beef jerky) or against the grain (which will be more tender). We recommend popping the steak in the freezer for 15-30 minutes before slicing so that it is easier to cut.
2. Transfer the strips of steak to a large ziplock bag.
3. In a separate small mixing bowl, whisk together the remaining ingredients until combined. Pour the mixture into the ziplock bag with the steak, seal the bag, and toss until the steak is evenly coated.
4. Refrigerate for at least 30 minutes or up to 1 day
5. To Dehydrate - Lay the strips out in a single layer on the trays. Dehydrate at 160 degrees for 4-6 hours depending on the thickness and desired texture. (But cooking times will vary based on the thickness of your meat).
6. Remove jerky and transfer to a sealed container. Refrigerate up to 1 month.

Crispy Air Fryer Bacon

Servings: 8

Ingredients:
- 3/4 lb. thick-cut bacon
- See All Nutritional Information

Directions:
1. Lay bacon inside air fryer basket in a single layer.
2. Set air fryer to 400° and cook until crispy, about 10 minutes. (You can check halfway through and rearrange slices with tongs.)

Bacon Wrapped Scallops

Ingredients:
- 12-15 scallops
- 1 lb. center cut bacon
- 6-8oz maple syrup
- 1 tsp garlic powder
- 1 tsp smoked paprika
- 1 tsp salt
- 1 tsp pepper
- 1/2 tsp rosemary

Directions:
1. Preheat the air fryer to 400F.
2. First, remove the muscle from each scallop.
3. Rinse each scallop and pat dry.
4. Wrap each scallops in bacon and secure with a toothpick.
5. Mix the maple syrup, garlic powder, paprika, salt, pepper and rosemary in a small bowl.
6. Generously baste the glaze onto each scallop.
7. Air fry for 12-14 minutes.
8. Remove to a decorative plate and serve immediately!

Air Fryer Meatloaf Recipe

Servings: 4
Cooking Time: 23 Minutes

Ingredients:
- FOR THE MEATLOAF:
- 1 medium yellow onion
- 2 cloves garlic
- 10 sprigs fresh parsley
- 1 large egg
- 2 tablespoons Worcestershire sauce
- 1 teaspoon kosher salt
- 1/2 teaspoon freshly ground black pepper
- 1/2 cup fine dry breadcrumbs
- 1 1/2 pounds ground beef
- FOR THE GLAZE:
- 1/4 cup ketchup
- 2 tablespoons spicy brown mustard

Directions:
1. Cut 1 medium yellow onion into 1-inch pieces. Place in a food processor fitted with the blade attachment and add 2 garlic cloves and the leaves from 10 fresh parsley sprigs. Pulse until finely chopped, 5 to 6 (1-second) pulses. (Alternatively, use the large holes on a box grater to grate the onion and a chef's knife to finely chop the garlic and parsley.) Transfer to a large bowl.
2. Add 1 large egg, 2 tablespoons Worcestershire sauce, 1 teaspoon kosher salt, and 1/2 teaspoon black pepper to the bowl, and stir to combine. Add 1/2 cup fine dry breadcrumbs and stir to combine. Add 1 1/2 pounds ground beef and mix with your hands until combined. Shape the mixture into 2 (3-inch wide, 6-inch long, and 1 1/2-inch high) loaves.
3. Heat an air fryer to 340F to 350F. Place the meatloaves in the air fryer side-by-side and air fry for 12 minutes. Meanwhile, make the glaze. Place 1/4 cup ketchup and 2 tablespoons spicy brown mustard in a small bowl, and stir to combine.
4. Flip the meatloaves over and air fry until the meatloaf darkens around the edges, about 8 minutes. Brush with half of the glaze. Air fry until an instant-read thermometer inserted into the center registers at least 165F and the glaze darkens slightly, 3 to 4 minutes more. Spoon the remaining glaze over the top of the meatloaves, slice, and serve.

RECIPE NOTES
Storage: Refrigerate leftovers in an airtight container for up to 3 days.

Lion's Head Chinese Meatballs

Servings: 5
Cooking Time: 20 Minutes

Ingredients:

- FOR THE MEATBALLS:
- 1 lb. ground pork
- 1/2 cup breadcrumbs
- 2 large eggs
- 2 tablespoons Shaoxing cooking wine (or mirin)
- 1/4 cup green onions, finely chopped
- 2 tablespoons soy sauce
- 1 teaspoon sesame oil
- 1/2 tablespoon brown sugar
- 1 teaspoon fresh ginger, grated
- 1 teaspoon garlic, minced
- 1 teaspoon salt
- 1/2 teaspoon ground black pepper (or white pepper)
- FOR THE SWEET SOY SAUCE:
- 1/4 cup soy sauce
- 1/4 cup chicken broth
- 2 tablespoons brown sugar
- 1 teaspoon sesame oil
- 1/2 tablespoon flour (or cornstarch)

Directions:

1. MAKE THE MEATBALLS:
2. In a large mixing bowl, combine pork with breadcrumbs, eggs, Shaoxing cooking wine, green onions, soy sauce, sesame oil, brown sugar, ginger, garlic, salt and pepper. Mix well until uniform in consistency.
3. Divide pork mixture into 5 equal pieces and roll into meatballs with your hands. Wear disposable gloves when handing meat to avoid contamination.
4. Cook the meatballs in the air fryer or oven.
5. In the air fryer: Place meatballs in a single layer in the air fryer and cook at 375F for 20 minutes, until the internal temperature reaches 160F when measured on a meat thermometer. Set aside.
6. In the oven: Place meatballs in a parchment-lined quarter sheet baking pan and cook in a 375 preheated oven for 40 minutes, until the internal temperature reaches 160F when measured on a meat thermometer. Set aside.
7. MAKE THE SWEET SOY SAUCE:
8. In a small mixing bowl, add soy sauce, chicken broth, brown sugar, sesame oil and flour. Whisk well to combine until flour and sugar dissolves.
9. Transfer the sauce into a shallow saucepan and heat over medium for 3-4 minutes. Continuously stir until desired consistency is reached.
10. Add meatballs to the saucepan and toss well to coat evenly. Garnish with green onions and serve warm with a bowl of steamed rice, and drizzle any extra sauce from the pan on top.

NOTES

How to store: Store lion's head meatballs in an airtight container and place in the refrigerator for up to 3 days. To reheat, simply reheat in a steamer or in a shallow saucepan on the stove over medium-low heat until warmed through. You may need to add a splash of water if the sauce thickened up too much in the refrigerator.

How to freeze uncooked meatballs: You can freeze uncooked lion's head meatballs by placing them on a quarter sheet baking pan lined with parchment paper. Then transfer to the freezer and freeze until hard, about 1 hour. Then, transfer the meatballs to a freezer bag or freezer-safe airtight container and store in the freezer for up to 3 months.

How to cook from frozen: Allow the meatballs to thaw overnight in the refrigerator first, then cook as per recipe instructions on the stove.

How to freeze cooked meatballs: Freeze cooled cooked meatballs by transferring into an airtight container or freezer bag. I would recommend freezing before mixing with the sauce, and making a fresh batch of sauce when ready to use.

Seared Steak With Truffle Herb Fries

Servings: 2
Cooking Time: 35 Minutes

Ingredients:
- SEARED STEAK
- 2 strip steaks
- kosher salt
- freshly cracked black pepper
- 3 to 4 tablespoons unsalted butter
- TRUFFLE HERB FRIES IN THE AIR FRYER
- 2 to 3 russet potatoes, thinly sliced
- olive oil for spritzing/brushing
- 1 teaspoon truffle salt
- 2 tablespoons chopped fresh parsley
- 2 tablespoons freshly grated parmesan cheese
- HONEY DIJON AIOLI
- ⅓ cup mayonnaise
- 1 garlic clove, minced
- 1 tablespoon dijon mustard
- 2 teaspoons honey

Directions:
1. SEARED STEAK
2. Make sure your steaks sit out at room temperature for about 30 minutes.
3. Heat a cast iron skillet over medium-high heat - you want it hot! Season the steaks on both sides with the salt and pepper.
4. Add 2 tablespoons of butter to the hot skillet. It will sizzle and smoke and once it's all melted, add in the steaks. Cook for 3 minute, until deeply golden, then flip and cook for 3 minutes more. Add in the remaining butter. Once it melts, spoon it over top of the steaks for another 1 to 2 minutes. I like to cook the steaks to about 140-145 degrees (almost medium doneness or medium well). Remove the steaks and let them rest for 10 to 15 minutes before slicing.
5. TRUFFLE HERB FRIES IN THE AIR FRYER
6. Place the sliced potatoes in a large bowl and cover with cold water. Let the potatoes sit in the water for 30 to 60 minutes. Remove the potatoes and place them on kitchen towels - you want them completely dry! Pat them as dry as you can!
7. Preheat your air fryer to 375 degrees F. Place the potatoes on a baking sheet and spray or brush with olive oil. Place the fries in a single layer in your air fryer (you might have to do 2 batches!). Cook for 12 minutes, then gently flip the fries and cook for 5 to 6 minutes more.
8. Stir together the parsley and parmesan cheese. When the fries are done, place them on a plate or a sheet of parchment paper and sprinkle all over with the truffle salt immediately. Sprinkle with the herbs and parmesan mixture. Serve with the aioli.
9. If you do 2 batches, or if the fries are done before the steak, you can stick these in a 200 degree F oven until ready to eat!
10. HONEY DIJON AIOLI
11. Whisk ingredients together until combined.

Air Fryer Bacon Wrapped Smokies

Servings: 4
Cooking Time: 12 Minutes

Ingredients:
- 1 package Little Smokies
- 1 pound bacon
- ½ cup brown sugar

Directions:
1. Cut bacon strips into thirds.
2. Wrap each smokie with a piece of bacon and then secure with a toothpick.
3. Add brown sugar to a large bowl. Toss bacon wrapped smokies with bacon, coating each piece.
4. Place smokies in the air fryer basket. Air fry at 380 degrees F for 10-12 minutes until bacon is crispy.

Ground Beef Tacos Recipe

Servings: 12
Cooking Time: 20 Minutes

Ingredients:
- 1 lb ground beef
- salt and pepper to taste
- 1 cup shredded mexican cheese
- 1-2 cups vegetable oil
- 12 yellow corn tortillas
- lettuce and tomato
- cooked cubed potatoes optional

Directions:
1. Cook the ground beef until browned. Season with salt and pepper. Drain, if needed.
2. Add meat and shredded cheese to a bowl and mix. (add the optional potatoes)
3. In a large frying pan heat up 1-1½ inches of vegetable oil.
4. Add about ⅓ cup of the meat mixture to the center of one tortilla. Fold the tortilla and clasp the top edges with tongs to keep it closed.
5. While holding the top of the tortilla place the bottom in the oil. Rock the tortilla from side to side a few times and then lie the tortilla on its side to fry.
6. Fry each side until golden brown and place on a plate lined with a paper towel to drain excess oil.
7. Fill each taco with lettuce and tomatoes before serving.

Roasted Cauliflower Steaks

Servings: 4
Cooking Time: 30 Minutes

Ingredients:
- 2 medium-large heads of cauliflower
- Marinade
- 2 tbsp oil
- 2 tbsp soy sauce (gluten-free if needed)
- 1 tbsp balsamic vinegar
- 1/2 tbsp maple syrup
- 3/4 tsp ground cumin
- 1/2 tsp smoked paprika
- Salt and pepper to taste
- Pinch of cayenne pepper (optional)
- Breading
- 1/2 cup (60 g) chickpea flour or oat flour
- 3 tbsp nutritional yeast
- 1 tsp paprika
- 1/2 tsp smoked paprika
- Salt and pepper

Directions:
1. You can watch the video in the post for visual instructions.
2. Trim the stem and remove the leaves from the cauliflower heads. Do not remove too much of the stem, otherwise, your "steaks" will fall apart.
3. With a large knife, cut the cauliflower lengthwise through the center into 1 1/2-inch (4 cm) thick pieces. Depending on the thickness of the stem you might end up with 2 or 3 "steaks". Don't throw away the little cauliflower pieces which aren't connected to the stem, use them as well to make cauliflower "wings".
4. Add some water with salt to a large pot and bring to a boil over high heat. Once the water boils, add the cauliflower, cover the pot and cook the cauliflower for 4-5 minutes to soften it a little. After 4-5 minutes, remove the cauliflower and set aside. You can also steam the cauliflower instead of cooking it.
5. In a small bowl mix together oil, soy sauce, balsamic vinegar, maple syrup, cumin, smoked paprika, salt, and pepper to taste.
6. Preheat oven to 410 degrees Fahrenheit (210 degrees Celsius) and line a large baking sheet with parchment paper.
7. Prepare the breading by simply mixing all ingredients (chickpea flour, nutritional yeast, paprika, smoked paprika, salt, and pepper) in a bowl with a whisk.
8. Place cauliflower steaks on the lined baking sheet. Brush with the marinade from all sides (see pictures above in the blog post).

9. Dip the cauliflower steaks in the breading and coat from all sides. Then spray with some cooking spray for a crispy breading.
10. Bake for about 25-30 minutes, or until golden brown, crispy, and fork-tender. Flip cauliflower steaks after 15-20 minutes.
11. Transfer to a platter and serve with fresh herbs, lemon juice, and your favorite dip. I made a cashew tahini dip (check the notes below for the recipe). Enjoy!

Notes

Enjoy the cauliflower steaks with this delicious tahini dressing.

Mix the ingredients for the dip in a small bowl with a whisk until creamy. If needed, add more water to thin out.

Recipe serves 4. Nutrition facts are for one serving.

Brussels & Bacon Flatbread

Ingredients:
- 4-6 slices thick-cut bacon, diced
- 8 ounces Brussels Sprouts, thinly-sliced
- 1/2 of a small red onion, thinly sliced
- 2 cloves garlic, minced
- 2 pieces flatbread (or store-bought naan)
- 1 tablespoon olive oil
- 1 cup Mozzarella cheese, shredded
- Crumbled feta cheese
- Balsamic glaze

Directions:
1. Line a sheet with parchment or foil and lay down the bacon slices. Cook at 350°F for about 10 minutes. Once bacon is at the desired crispiness, set aside to cool.
2. Once the bacon is cooled and able to be handled, dice it into small pieces.
3. Place the piece of flatbread on the 12" circular pizza pan, and brush the top with olive oil. Sprinkle evenly with about 1/3 of the Mozzarella cheese, leaving a 1/2-inch border around the edges of the flatbread. Then add the brussels, red onion, bacon, 1 clove of minced garlic and the crumbled cheese. Finish with a sprinkle more of the

mozzarella cheese. Repeat all steps with the second pizza.
4. Bake at 350°F for 8-10 minutes, or until the Mozzarella has melted and the crusts are slightly golden.
5. Remove from the oven and drizzle with the balsamic glaze. Serve immediately.

Frozen Pork Chops In The Air Fryer

Servings: 4
Cooking Time: 15 Minutes

Ingredients:
- 4 1-inch thick boneless pork chops, frozen
- 1 ½ teaspoons smoked paprika
- 1 teaspoon brown sugar
- ½ teaspoon kosher salt
- ½ teaspoon black pepper
- ¼ teaspoon onion powder
- ¼ teaspoon garlic powder
- ⅛ teaspoon cayenne pepper

Directions:
1. Preheat your air fryer to 380 degrees F.
2. Place the frozen chops in the air fryer in a single layer. Defrost the chops in the air fryer for 5 minutes.
3. While the chops defrost, mix together the remaining ingredients in a small bowl.
4. When the timer is done, open the basket and remove the chops to a cutting board. Spray them with cooking spray, then sprinkle the dry rub on all over the chops.
5. Return the chops to the fryer basket and continue cooking for 12-18 minutes (depending on the thickness of your chops), or until the middle is no longer pink, and reads 145 degrees F when probed with a meat thermometer.
6. Allow the chops to rest for 5 minutes before serving.

NOTES
HOW TO REHEAT PORK CHOPS IN THE AIR FRYER:
Preheat your air fryer to 350 degrees.
Place the leftover pork chops in the air fryer and cook for 3 to 5 minutes, until they're thoroughly warmed.

Air Fryer Bbq Pork Tenderloin

Servings: 4

Cooking Time: 20 Minutes

Ingredients:

- 10 ounces pork tenderloin cut into two pieces
- 1 cup BBQ Sauce any type

Directions:

1. Set it in the air fryer oven or basket and set the temperature to 400 degrees F, air fryer setting, for 5 minutes.
2. Brush the BBQ sauce on the pork tenderloin, and air fry for another 10 to 15 minutes.
3. Check the internal temperature. Once it reaches: 145 degrees F, remove. Let rest for about 5 minutes before you cut into it. That will allow the juices to settle inside.
4. Plate, serve, and enjoy!

Air Fryer Twice-baked Potatoes With Kale, Ham & Goat's Cheese

Servings: 2

Cooking Time: 50 Minutes

Ingredients:

- 2 large baking potatoes
- 1 tbsp olive oil
- 200g pack thick cut cavolo nero
- 1 clove/s small garlic, crushed
- 1/2 x 180g Cooks' Ingredients Smoked Ham Batons
- 75g soft goat's cheese
- 4 salad onions, trimmed and finely sliced
- 200g Bellaverde sweet stem broccoli, trimmed

Directions:

1. Turn the air fryer to 190°C and make sure the grate is inserted in the base of the bowl. Rub the potatoes with ½ tbsp oil and season. Make a small slit in the top of each potato and put them on top of the grate. Cook for 40 minutes, turning halfway, until crisp, golden brown and tender in the centre when tested with a knife.
2. Remove the potatoes from the air fryer and, in a large bowl, use your hands to scrunch the cavolo nero with the remaining ½ tbsp oil and the garlic; season. Tip into the air fryer and cook for 4 minutes, stirring halfway, until just beginning to crisp at the edges.
3. Set half the cavolo nero aside and tip the remainder back into the large bowl. Cut the top off each potato and carefully scoop the flesh into the bowl, leaving a border of about 1cm. Add the flesh from the 'lids' too, then discard the skins from the tops. Add the ham, goat's cheese and salad onions, roughly mashing the mixture with a fork. Spoon the filling into the skins and cook in the air fryer for a final 5 minutes.
4. Meanwhile, steam the broccoli for 3-4 minutes until tender or cook in the air fryer (see intro). Once the potatoes are cooked, transfer them to warm serving plates and return the reserved cavolo nero to the air fryer for 1-2 minutes to heat through. Toss with the broccoli and serve alongside the stuffed potatoes.

Cook's tip

Customer safety tips

Follow manufacturer's instructions and advice for specific foods

Pre-heat the air fryer to the correct temperature

If cooking different foods together, be aware that they may require different times and temperatures

Spread food evenly – do not overcrowd pan/chamber

Turn food midway through cooking

Check food is piping/steaming hot and cooked all the way through

Aim for golden colouring – do not overcook

VEGETABLE & & VEGETARIAN RECIPES

Air Fryer Sweet Potatoes

Servings: 4
Cooking Time: 20 Minutes

Ingredients:

- 2 lb Sweet potatoes (4-5 medium, unpeeled)
- 2 tbsp Olive oil (or avocado oil)
- 1 tsp Dried oregano
- 1 tsp Garlic powder
- 1/2 tsp Paprika
- 3/4 tsp Sea salt (plus more to taste at the end)
- 1/4 tsp Black pepper (plus more to taste at the end)

Directions:

1. Wash the potatoes and pat dry with paper towels (drying is important so they can get crispy). Cut into wedges of similar size.
2. In a large bowl, combine the sweet potato wedges, olive oil, and seasonings. Toss to coat.
3. Arrange the sweet potato wedges in the air fryer basket in a single layer, leaving space between them. (Cook in batches if needed to avoid crowding the basket; mine required 3 batches.)
4. Cook sweet potatoes in the air fryer at 390 degrees F (199 degrees C) for 20-25 minutes, shaking the air fryer basket every 8-10 minutes, until golden and crisp.
5. Remove the basket and sprinkle the wedges with additional salt and pepper to taste.

Garlic Mashed Potatoes

Servings: 4-6
Cooking Time: 40 Minutes

Ingredients:

- 1 head garlic, whole and unpeeled
- 1 tablespoon extra virgin olive oil
- 2 pounds potatoes, preferably Yukon Gold or another yellow, waxy potato
- 1/2 teaspoon salt , plus more to taste
- 1/3 cup cream
- 3 tablespoons butter

Directions:

1. Preheat the oven:
2. Preheat the oven to 400°F.
3. Roast the garlic:
4. Remove the outer layer of papery skin of the whole garlic head, leaving the head itself intact.
5. Using a paring knife, slice off the tops (1/4 to 1/2 inch) of the garlic cloves so they are all exposed. Place the garlic head on a piece of aluminum foil. Drizzle olive oil over the garlic head, salt lightly, and wrap the foil lightly around the garlic.
6. Bake at 400°F for 30 to 40 minutes, or until the cloves feel soft to the touch and are beginning to brown. Remove from the oven and let cool.
7. Boil the potatoes:
8. While the garlic is roasting, peel and chop the potatoes into 1-inch chunks. Place potatoes in a medium saucepan, add 1/2 teaspoon salt, cover with cold water.
9. Bring the pot to a boil, reduce to a simmer, and simmer potatoes until tender when pierced with a fork, about 15 minutes.
10. Warm the cream and melt the butter:
11. Either in a small pan on the stovetop or in a bowl in the microwave, combine the cream and butter. Cook over low heat until the butter is melted and the cream is warmed through.
12. Mash the potatoes with garlic:
13. Drain the pot with the potatoes and put it back on the stovetop over low heat. Put the drained potatoes back in the pot.
14. Squeeze the roasted garlic into the potatoes and begin mashing with a potato masher or a large fork.
15. Add the cream and butter, then season:
16. Add the cream and butter and mash until the potatoes are the consistency you want. Do not over-beat them, or the potatoes will become gummy.
17. Taste for salt and add some more, if needed.

Air Fryer Roasted Potatoes Recipe

Servings: 4

Cooking Time: 20 Minutes

Ingredients:

- 1 pound baby Yukon Gold potatoes (about 1-inch wide)
- 1 tablespoon olive oil
- 2 teaspoons Italian seasoning
- 1/2 teaspoon garlic powder
- 1/2 teaspoon kosher salt
- 1/4 teaspoon freshly ground black pepper

Directions:

1. Heat an air fryer to 400°F. Meanwhile, halve 1 pound baby Yukon Gold potatoes and place in a medium bowl. Add 1 tablespoon olive oil, 2 teaspoons Italian seasoning, 1/2 teaspoon garlic powder, 1/2 teaspoon kosher salt, and 1/4 teaspoon black pepper, and toss to coat.
2. Arrange the potatoes in an even layer in the air fryer basket or tray (air fry in batches if needed). Air fry until lightly browned with crispy edges, tossing halfway through, about 20 minutes total.
3. NOTES
4. Storage: Refrigerate in an airtight container for up to 4 days.

Two Mushroom Risotto

Servings: 2

Ingredients:

- 160g chestnut mushrooms
- 30ml Chinese rice wine sachet
- 1 spring onion
- 5g chives
- 150g portobello mushrooms
- 1 veg stock cube
- 40g cheddar cheese
- 160g arborio rice
- 3 garlic clove
- 40g Cornish clotted cream

Directions:

1. Boil a kettle and trim and finely slice the spring onion. Then chop the chives finely and peel and finely chop (or grate) the garlic. Dissolve the veg stock cube in 650ml boiled water
2. Add a drizzle of vegetable oil to the air fryer, tear and crumble both the portobello and chestnut mushrooms directly into the air fryer. Cook at 200c for 3-5 min or until starting to brown and caramelise
3. Once caramelised, transfer the mushrooms to a bowl and cover to keep warm. Add the sliced spring onion and half of the chopped chives (save the rest for garnish!) with a knob of butter to the air fryer along with the arborio rice, chopped garlic and Chinese rice wine stir to combine.
4. Add the vegetable stock and return to the air fryer cook for 30 -35 mins, stirring every 5 minutes until all the stock is absorbed and the rice is cooked – this is your risotto
5. Meanwhile, grate the cheddar cheese.
6. Once the risotto is cooked, stir in the grated cheese, clotted cream and half of the mushrooms (save the other half for garnish!) Add a little more boiled water if your risotto is too clumpy – a risotto should have an almost porridge-like consistency.
7. Season with pepper and serve the risotto in bowls and top with the remaining mushrooms, a sprinkle of the remaining chives and a good grind of black pepper

Popcorn Vegan Pieces With Buffalo Sauce

Servings: 2

Ingredients:

- 1 pack Quorn Vegan Pieces
- 2 tsp smoked paprika
- 1 tsp brown sugar
- 1 tsp cornflour
- 1 tsp onion powder
- 1 tsp garlic powder
- 100ml Aquafaba (liquid from drained tin of chickpeas)
- 40g panko breadcrumbs
- 1 tbsp dried thyme
- 1/2 tsp salt
- For the Buffalo Sauce

- 1 tbsp maple sauce
- 1 tbsp sriracha chilli sauce
- 1 tbsp apple cider vinegar

Directions:
1. Preheat air fryer to 180C, we used the Ninja Foodi Dual Zone Air Fryer. Line a large baking tray or chopping board with baking paper
2. Combine the paprika, sugar, cornflour, onion powder and garlic powder in a medium shallow dish. Add the frozen Quorn Vegan Pieces, a few pieces at a time, and stir to coat. Transfer to the prepared tray
3. Drain the chickpeas and keep for another meal, reserve the chickpea water (aka Aquafaba). Add the coated pieces, a few pieces at a time, and stir to coat. Return pieces to the tray
4. Combine the panko breadcrumbs and thyme in another medium shallow dish. Add the pieces, a few pieces a time, and turn to coat
5. Line your air fryer drawer with baking paper (use both drawer zones if using Ninja Foodi Dual Zone Air Fryer). Place crumbed pieces inside. Select Air Fry and set time to 10 minutes. Press Start/Stop to begin. Fry for 10 minutes or until the crust is golden
6. While the pieces are cooking, make the buffalo sauce by placing all ingredients into a small serving bowl and whisk to combine
7. Transfer the pieces onto a serving plate. Sprinkle with cracked black pepper & thyme and drizzle over a little buffalo sauce. Serve with remaining sauce

Air Fryer Frozen Vegetables

Servings: 4
Cooking Time: 10 Minutes

Ingredients:
- 16 ounces frozen vegetables
- 1 tablespoon olive oil
- ½ teaspoon salt
- ½ teaspoon pepper

Directions:
1. Preheat air fryer to 400°F.
2. Toss frozen vegetables with the olive oil and seasonings.
3. Spread the vegetables out evenly into the air fryer basket and cook for 10 minutes, shaking the basket halfway through cooking.

Notes
Always preheat the air fryer so the blast of hot air circulates around the veggies, making them tender and crispy.

Mashed Potato Balls

Servings: 20
Cooking Time: 15 Minutes

Ingredients:
- 3 cups leftover mashed potatoes
- 1/2 cup cheddar cheese, shredded
- 1/4 cup green onions, finely chopped
- 1 teaspoon garlic powder
- 1/2 teaspoon paprika
- 1/2 teaspoon salt (or to taste)
- 1/4 teaspoon ground black pepper (or to taste)
- 2 cups panko breadcrumbs
- vegetable oil (for frying)

Directions:
1. In a large mixing bowl, add mashed potatoes, cheese, green onions, garlic powder, paprika, salt and pepper. Mix well until smooth.
2. Take 2 tablespoons of the potato mixture at a time and shape into balls by hand, similar to shaping meatballs. Alternatively, you can use a cookie scoop to shape into even pieces.
3. Add breadcrumbs in a large bowl. Dip the mashed potato balls in crumbs and gently press crumbs around each ball to coat.
4. Arrange the coated mashed potato balls evenly on a parchment-lined half sheet baking pan and transfer into the freezer. Freeze for 15-20 minutes to firm up. This helps the mashed potato bites hold their shape when deep-frying.

5. Add 2-inches of oil into a cooking pot and heat over medium-high heat until shimmering hot, about 3-4 minutes. Add the potato balls in batches (about 4-5 pieces each time) until crisp and golden brown, about 1-2 minutes. Turn the balls occasionally to get an even golden crust on all sides.
6. Transfer the potato balls to a paper towel lined plate to drain excess oil, and let them cool for 5 minutes before serving.

NOTES

How to cook in the air fryer: Preheat the air fryer to 375 F, about 3 minutes. Carefully place mashed potato in a single layer in the air fryer basket and lightly spray with cooking oil to coat evenly. Air fry the mashed potato bites for 10-15 minutes until golden brown. Gently shake the basket halfway during cooking to brown evenly.

How to freeze: I recommend freezing these mashed potato balls before you cook them. Prepare them up to the point of frying, then arrange the balls in a single layer on a large half sheet baking pan. Freeze until hard, about 1 hour. Then transfer to a freezer bag or airtight container and freeze for up to 3 months.

How to cook from frozen: Cook in the same way that you would when following the recipe. It will take a few minutes longer to cook until crisp and golden brown.

How to store: Make sure the fried mashed potato balls cool to room temperature completely before storing. Skipping this step can result in soggy potato bites. Then, transfer the balls to an airtight container and refrigerate for up to 4-5 days.

How to reheat: Reheat leftover mashed potato balls in a 375F oven for 15-20 minutes, or air fryer for 10 minutes.

Make ahead instructions: If you want to prep these mashed potato balls ahead of time, make them the day or morning before and store them in the freezer. Then, when it's time to serve, quickly fry them up. You could also cook them in advance, refrigerate, and pop into the oven to reheat.

Air Fryer Baked Potatoes

Servings: 4
Cooking Time: 55 Minutes

Ingredients:
- 4 medium russet potatoes
- 1 tablespoon olive oil
- ½ teaspoon salt or to taste

Directions:
1. Scrub potatoes and towel dry. Poke each potato with a fork several times.
2. Rub the outside of the potato with oil and season with salt.
3. Place in the air fryer at 390°F and cook for 25 minutes. Flip the potatoes and cook for an additional 20-30 minutes or until tender when pierced with a fork.
4. Serve with desired toppings.

Spiced Butternut Squash

Servings: 2

Ingredients:
- 1 large Butternut Squash, peeled and cut into wedges
- 2 tbsp Olive Oil
- 1 tbsp Garlic Paste
- 1 tsp Onion Powder
- 1 tsp dry Oregano
- 1 tsp smoked Paprika
- 1 tsp Cayenne Pepper
- 1 tsp Salt
- 1/2 - 1 tsp Black Pepper

Directions:
1. Preheat the air fryer to 200C.
2. Place the Squash in a large bowl.
3. Add Oil, Garlic, Onion Powder, Oregano, Paprika, Cayenne, Salt and Pepper.
4. Toss to coat.
5. Place squash in the Air Fryer basket for 15 – 20 minutes. Shake every 5 minutes.

Air Fryer Grilled Tomato And Cheese

Servings: 2
Cooking Time: 9 Minutes

Ingredients:
- 4 slices sourdough bread
- 4 slices tomato
- 1 cup Gruyere cheese shredded
- 1 teaspoon basalmic vinegar
- 1 Tablespoon unsalted butter melted

Directions:
1. Spread a light coat of butter onto both sides of each slice of bread.
2. Assemble each sandwich by adding slices of tomato, ½ cup shredded Gruyere cheese, and then brushing the tomatoes with the balsamic vinegar.
3. Place prepared sandwiches in a single layer into the basket of the air fryer.
4. Air fry the tomato and cheese sandwiches at 370 degrees Fahrenheit for 8-10 minutes, flipping halfway through. Remove from the air fryer when they've reached your preferred level of golden, crispy brown.

NOTES

This recipe was made in the 1700 watt 5.8 quart basket style Cosori air fryer. If you are using a different size or different brand of air fryer, you may need to adjust the cooking time slightly. All air fryers will cook a little differently.

Consider using different cheeses such as American, Provolone, or Swiss cheese to change the flavors.

Air-fryer General Tso's Cauliflower

Servings: 4
Cooking Time: 20 Minutes

Ingredients:
- 1/2 cup all-purpose flour
- 1/2 cup cornstarch
- 1 teaspoon salt
- 1 teaspoon baking powder
- 3/4 cup club soda
- 1 medium head cauliflower, cut into 1-inch florets (about 6 cups)
- SAUCE:
- 1/4 cup orange juice
- 3 tablespoons sugar
- 3 tablespoons soy sauce
- 3 tablespoons vegetable broth
- 2 tablespoons rice vinegar
- 2 teaspoons sesame oil
- 2 teaspoons cornstarch
- 2 tablespoons canola oil
- 2 to 6 dried pasilla or other hot chiles, chopped
- 3 green onions, white part minced, green part thinly sliced
- 3 garlic cloves, minced
- 1 teaspoon grated fresh gingerroot
- 1/2 teaspoon grated orange zest
- 4 cups hot cooked rice

Directions:
1. Preheat air fryer to 400°. Combine flour, cornstarch, salt and baking powder. Stir in club soda just until blended (batter will be thin). Toss florets in batter; transfer to a wire rack set over a baking sheet. Let stand 5 minutes. In batches, place cauliflower on greased tray in air-fryer basket. Cook until golden brown and tender, 10-12 minutes.
2. Meanwhile, whisk together first 6 sauce ingredients; whisk in cornstarch until smooth.
3. In a large saucepan, heat canola oil over medium-high heat. Add chiles; cook and stir until fragrant, 1-2 minutes. Add white part of onions, garlic, ginger and orange zest; cook until fragrant, about 1 minute. Stir orange juice mixture; add to saucepan. Bring to a boil; cook and stir until thickened, 2-4 minutes.
4. Add cauliflower to sauce; toss to coat. Serve with rice; sprinkle with thinly sliced green onions.

Crispy Air Fryer Roasted Brussels Sprouts With Balsamic

Servings: 4

Cooking Time: 15 Minutes

Ingredients:

- 1 pound brussels sprouts , ends removed and cut into bite sized pieces
- 2 Tablespoons olive oil , or more if needed
- 1 Tablespoon balsamic vinegar
- kosher salt , to taste
- black pepper , to taste

Directions:

1. Put cut brussels sprouts to bowl. Drizzle oil and balsamic vinegar evenly over the brussels sprouts. Don't dump the oil and vinegar in one spot or else it will just coat one brussels sprout. You want to make sure to coat all the brussels sprouts.
2. Sprinkle salt and pepper evenly over the brussels sprouts. Stir to combine everything and long enough so that all the brussels sprouts soaks up the marinade. There shouldn't be any marinade left in the bottom of the bowl.
3. Add brussels to the air fryer basket. Air fry at 360°F for about 15-20 minutes. Shake and gently stir half way through, about 8 minutes into cooking. Make sure you shake at the halfway mark! You don't wany to end up with uneven cooking. If needed, shake and toss a 3rd time to make sure it all cooks evenly.
4. Continue to air fry the brussels for the remainder of the time, or until the brussels are golden brown and cooked through. You can check earlier if needed to make sure nothing burns. Or you can add more time if needed to make sure it's cooked through.
5. Add additional salt and pepper if needed on the brussels sprouts and enjoy!

NOTES

Don't crowd the basket. If needed, it's better to cook in multiple smaller batches for even cooking, than it is to cook in one large batch. If cooking in multiple batches, the first batch will take longer to cook if Air Fryer is not already pre-heated.

If you decide to double the recipe, it will work great but make sure your air fryer is large enough (this recipe was cooked in a 3.7 qt air fryer). You might need add an additional 1-2 minutes of cooking time and give an extra shake or two while cooking if the basket is fairly full. Remember to set a timer to shake/flip/toss the food as directed in recipe.

Air Fryer Asparagus

Servings: 4

Cooking Time: 6 Minutes

Ingredients:

- 1 pound asparagus
- 2 teaspoons olive oil
- salt & pepper to taste

Directions:

1. Rinse asparagus and dry well. Holding the center and bottom of each spear, snap off the bottom and discard.
2. Preheat air fryer to 400°F.
3. Toss asparagus with olive oils and season with salt & pepper.
4. Cook 6-10 minutes* or until tender-crisp and lightly roasted.

Notes

Cook Time: Thinner asparagus will take closer to 6 minutes and thicker stalks will take closer to 10 minutes.

Oven Baked Fingerling Potatoes

Servings: 4

Cooking Time: 20 Minutes

Ingredients:

- 1 pound fingerling potatoes cut in half lengthwise
- 2 tablespoons olive oil
- 2 cloves garlic minced
- 1 teaspoon salt
- ¼ teaspoon dried thyme leaves or 2 sprigs fresh thyme

- 1 teaspoon pepper
- 1 tablespoon parmesan cheese shredded

Directions:
1. Preheat oven to 400°F.
2. In a large bowl, combine potatoes, oil, garlic, salt, pepper, and thyme. Toss until evenly coated.
3. Spread onto a baking sheet flat side down and bake for 15 minutes.
4. Remove from the oven and sprinkle parmesan cheese on top, return to the oven and cook for another 10-15 minutes or until potatoes are golden brown in color.

Notes

In the Air Fryer: Preheat the air fryer to 400°F. Cut the potatoes, coat with spices and oil. Place in the air fryer. Cook for 7 minutes. Sprinkle with parmesan and cook for another 8 minutes.

Mixed Mediterranean Veggies With Vinaigrette

Servings: 4

Ingredients:
- 1 red pepper, cut in 3cm slices
- 1 yellow pepper, cut in 3cm slices
- 2 medium courgettes, cut in 2cm slices
- 1 medium red onion, peeled and petals cut in 5cm pieces
- 5 garlic cloves, peeled and minced
- 2 tbsp olive oil, divided
- Flaked sea salt, to taste
- Fresh cracked black pepper, to taste
- 1 tsp red wine vinegar
- 1 tbsp capers
- 1/4 tsp chilli flakes
- Fresh torn basil

Directions:
1. Insert crisper plate in pan and place pan in unit. Preheat unit by selecting AIR FRY, set temperature to 180°C and set time to 3 minutes. Select START/STOP to begin.
2. In a large bowl, combine red pepper, yellow pepper, courgettes, red onion, garlic, 1 tablespoon olive oil, sea salt and black pepper. Mix well.
3. Once unit has preheated, remove pan and add vegetables to crisping plate. Place pan back in unit and select AIR FRY. Set temperature to 180°C, set time for 15 minutes and select START/ STOP to begin.
4. When cooking is complete, remove pan and place cooked vegetables in a large bowl with vinegar, remaining oil, capers, chilli flakes and basil. Mix well to combine, adjusting seasoning as desired.

Air Fryer Corn On The Cob

Servings: 4
Cooking Time: 15 Minutes

Ingredients:
- 4 ears of corn
- 1 Tablespoon olive oil
- salt and pepper

Directions:
1. Place the corn in the basket of the air fryer. Rub the olive oil evenly on the corn. Add salt and pepper.
2. Cook in the air fryer at 370 degrees for 12-15 minutes or until tender.

Easy Air Fryer Baked Potatoes

Servings: 4
Cooking Time: 40 Minutes

Ingredients:
- 4 large baking potatoes, scrubbed
- 2 tablespoons olive oil
- kosher salt and freshly ground black pepper to taste
- ½ teaspoon garlic powder, or to taste
- ½ teaspoon dried parsley, or to taste
- 4 tablespoons butter

Directions:
1. Preheat an air fryer to 400 degrees F (200 degrees C).

2. Rub potatoes with olive oil and season with salt, pepper, garlic powder, and parsley. Place potatoes in the air fryer basket.
3. Cook in the preheated air fryer until potatoes are soft, 40 to 50 minutes, depending on potato size.
4. Slice potatoes lengthwise. Pinch both sides of each potato, using your hands and forcing potatoes to open, until the fluffy insides start to come out. Add 1 tablespoon of butter into each potato.

Air Fryer Stuffed Peppers

Servings: 4
Cooking Time: 15 Minutes

Ingredients:
- 4-6 Bell Peppers destemed and seeds removed
- 15 oz diced tomatoes
- 15 oz tomato sauce
- 1 cup cooked rice
- 1 can kidney beans drained and rinsed
- 1-2 T Italian Seasoning
- 1/2 cup mozzarella cheese
- 1 T parmesan cheese

Directions:
1. Remove tops from bell peppers. Deseed and scoop them out. Take the tops (lids of bell peppers) and dice up.
2. Combine diced bell pepper tops, diced tomatoes (with juice), rice, beans and seasoning together.
3. Place mixture into scooped out bell peppers. Fill bell peppers almost to top with mixture.
4. Placed stuffed peppers into air fryer basket. Cook at 360 degrees F for 12 minutes. Remove from air fryer but keep in basket.
5. Top the air fryer stuffed peppers with cheese mixture and cook for another 3 minutes at 360 degrees F or until cheese is melted. ENJOY!

Notes
Depending on the size of your bell peppers, you may be able to adjust the recipe. For example: if you are using smaller bell peppers you will be able to use more peppers with the amount of mixture!
If you are using bigger bell peppers you might need to increase the cook time.

Air Fry Crumbed Cauliflower Bites With Yogurt Dip

Servings: 4
Cooking Time: 12 Minutes

Ingredients:
- 1 head of cauliflower
- ½ cup flour (can be gluten free)
- 2 eggs
- 1 cup breadcrumbs
- 1 tsp chopped parsley
- ¼ tsp fresh thyme leaves
- ¼ tsp paprika
- ¼ tsp salt
- Zest 1 lemon
- 2 Tbls grated parmesan (optional)
- ½ tsp chilli flakes (optional)
- 1 Tbls olive oil

Directions:
1. Cut the cauliflower into bite size florets.
2. Mix the breadcrumbs, herbs, paprika, salt, lemon zest, chilli and parmesan together.
3. Whisk the eggs.
4. Toss the cauliflower in flour then dip into the egg mix then coat in the crumbs.
5. Drizzle the crumbed cauliflower with olive oi.l
6. Set the Vortex (or Duo Crisp) to Air Fry at 180c for 12 mins, it will start to Pre Heat.
7. Once the Vortex (or Duo Crisp) beeps, "add food", place cauliflower inside the basket.
8. The Vortex (or Duo Crisp) will beep and prompt you to turn the cauliflower halfway through cooking.
9. Serve with garlic & herb garlic dip.
10. Garlic & herb yogurt dip:
11. 1 cup plain yogurt
12. 1 clove garlic
13. Pinch chilli flakes
14. ¼ cup chopped herbs (parsley, coriander, chives)

15. Black pepper
16. Mix all the ingredients together.
NOTES
Set up an olive or avocado oil spritz bottle (as used for salad dressings) to use to coat the ingredients before air frying. Avoid the traditional non-stick sprays which contain soya lecithin as these may damage the non-stick coatings.

Sweet Chilli Tofu With Roasted Cauliflower & Broccoli

Servings: 3

Ingredients:
- For the veg mix
- 1 cauliflower
- 1 broccoli
- 1 tbsp chilli oil
- 1 tsp salt
- 1 tsp black pepper
- For the tofu
- 280g block tofu, drained and cubed
- 1 tbsp chilli oil
- 1/2 tsp ground ginger
- 1/2 tsp garlic powder
- 1/2 tsp chilli powder
- 1/2 tsp sea salt
- 5 tbsp sweet chilli sauce, some for glaze

Directions:
1. Prep the veg by washing and cutting the cauliflower and broccoli into bite size pieces
2. Place in a bowl and add the chilli oil, salt and black pepper. Mix until the broccoli and cauliflower is covered
3. Add this to tray 1 of the Ninja Foodi Dual Zone Air Fryer
4. Add the tofu into a bowl, add the oil and then the seasoning. Mix until all combined
5. Add this to tray 2 of the Ninja Foodi Dual Zone Air Fryer
6. Press 1 on the Ninja Foodi Dual Zone Air Fryer. Press roast, set the temp to 180c and the time to 12 mins
7. Press 2 on the Ninja Foodi Dual Zone Air Fryer. Press air fry, set the temp to 190c and the time to 18mins. Press SYNC and then START

Air Fryer Eggplant Parm

Servings: 2-4

Ingredients:
- 4 slices crusty white bread, torn into small pieces (about 1 c.)
- 1 clove garlic, minced
- 1 tbsp. plus 2 tsp. extra-virgin olive oil
- Kosher salt
- 1 small Italian eggplant (about 1 lb.), trimmed, sliced crosswise 1/2"-thick
- Freshly ground black pepper
- 3/4 c. marinara sauce
- 3/4 c. shredded mozzarella
- 1/4 c. packed fresh basil leaves

Directions:
1. In a medium bowl, toss bread, garlic, and 2 tsp. oil; season with salt. In an air-fryer basket, arrange bread in a single layer. Cook at 370°, tossing a few times, until golden and crisp, about 3 minutes. Transfer to a plate. Wipe basket clean.
2. Season eggplant with 1/2 teaspoon salt and a few grinds of pepper. Brush cut sides with remaining 1 tbsp. oil.
3. Working in batches, in air-fryer basket, arrange eggplant in a single layer, spacing about 1/4" apart. Cook at 400°, flipping halfway through, until very tender and golden, about 12 minutes. Spoon some marinara on top of slices; top with some mozzarella. Return to air fryer and continue to cook until cheese is melted and bubbly, 1 to 2 minutes more.
4. Divide eggplant among plates. Top with basil and bread crumbs.

Air Fryer Corn

Servings: 2
Cooking Time: 13 Minutes

Ingredients:

- 2 ears of corn
- 2 tablespoons butter
- 1/2 teaspoon dried parsley (or 1 1/2 teaspoon fresh)
- 1/4 teaspoon sea salt
- 2 tablespoons shredded Parmesan cheese (or grated)

Directions:

1. Preheat your air fryer to 400 degrees.
2. Shuck both ears of corn and remove any silk. Cut corns in half if desired.
3. Mix together melted butter, parsley, and sea salt in a bowl. Baste on corn evenly.
4. Place corn inside the air fryer side by side and cook for 12-14 minutes until some pieces are browned.
5. Remove the corn from the air fryer and roll in the Parmesan cheese.
6. Enjoy immediately or place in the fridge for up to 3 days without cheese on top.

Air Fryer Broccoli And Carrots

Servings: 2
Cooking Time: 10 Minutes

Ingredients:

- 1 head broccoli rinsed
- 12 ounces carrots washed and peeled
- 2 Tablespoons olive oil
- 2 cloves garlic minced
- 1 teaspoon kosher salt
- 1/2 teaspoon ground black pepper

Directions:

1. Cut, peel, and wash carrots into ½-inch angled slices.
2. Cut the head of the broccoli into bite-sized florets.
3. Add broccoli and carrots into a large mixing bowl.
4. Add in the tablespoons of olive oil/avocado oil, minced garlic, salt, and black pepper. Mix together till the broccoli and carrots are coated.
5. Transfer the seasoned vegetables to the air fryer basket and cook at 390F for 10 minutes flipping halfway through. You will have to do these in batches. Also make sure the carrots are in a single layer and not stacked on top of each other.
6. Remove from the air fryer basket and serve.
NOTES
If you don't have regular carrots, baby carrots can be substituted. Make sure to cut them in half at a diagonal.
If I'm running short on time, I love to prep veggies earlier in the day and save them until I make the meal.

Air Fryer Sliced Potatoes

Servings: 4
Cooking Time: 15 Minutes

Ingredients:

- 1 pound yellow potatoes, peeled and sliced into ¼" slices
- 1 tablespoon oil
- ½ teaspoon salt
- ¼ teaspoon garlic powder
- ¼ teaspoon black pepper
- Fresh parsley for garnish (optional)

Directions:

1. Preheat your air fryer to 380 F.
2. Toss the potato slices with the oil, salt, garlic powder, and pepper.
3. Spread the potatoes as evenly as possible in the basket, then cook for 15 minutes, flipping once halfway through.
4. Serve immediately.

FAVORITE AIR FRYER RECIPES

Mama Sue's Salsa

Ingredients:

- 28 oz. can diced tomatoes
- 3 stalks green onion, cut into thirds
- 10-12 stalks cilantro (leaves only), cut into thirds
- 1 jalapeno
- 1 lime, cut in half and juiced
- 1 tsp pepper
- 1 tsp seasoned salt
- 1 tsp coriander
- 1 tsp chili powder
- 1 tsp garlic salt

Directions:

1. Roughly chop the green onion and cilantro.
2. Slice your jalapeno in half. To change the level of heat in your salsa, then add or take away the seeds.
3. Cut your lime in half.
4. Drain half of the juice from the canned tomatoes and discard.
5. In your blender, add in the cilantro, green onions, jalapenos and remaining tomato juice. Squeeze in as much lime as desired. Place the lid on and pulse until chopped semi-finely.
6. Add in the diced tomatoes, spices and desired level of jalapeno seeds. *If you decide after you've added the jalapeno seeds, that you want a little more spice, then feel free to add chili pepper or paprika!
7. Pulse until you get your desired consistency. Serve at room temperature with your favorite tortilla chips. Enjoy!
8. *make homemade tortilla chips in an air fryer to go with salsa. They only need a couple minutes in the air fryer and you've got a crispy side to go along with it!

Air Fryer Churro Bites

Ingredients:

- 1 CUP water
- 1/2 CUP unsalted butter
- 1/4 TSP salt
- 1 CUP all purpose flour
- 3 eggs
- 1/4 sugar
- Pastry piping bag and star tip

Directions:

1. In a pot on your stovetop, bring the water to a boil, and drop in butter. Turn off heat and stir in salt, flour and eggs. Mix well until it balls up.
2. Using a pastry piping bag, transfer the dough into the pastry piping bag and attach the star tip. carefully squeeze mini sized portions, about 1.5 inches logo on the baking pan.
3. Transfer the baking pan onto the rack in the Turbo air fryer, and set it to 410F degrees and fry for 6 minutes.
4. Pour the 1/4 cup sugar into a small bowl, then roll the air fried churros in the sugar and serve.

Air Fryer Fried Tagalongs

Servings: 4
Cooking Time: 5 Minutes

Ingredients:

- 4 Tagalongs
- 4 Crescent dough sheets
- powdered sugar

Directions:

1. Preheat the Air Fryer to 360 degrees Fahrenheit. Prepare the basket with nonstick spray if needed.
2. Unwrap the crescent rolls dough sheets and set them aside.
3. Place a Tagalong cookie onto the crescent dough sheet and cover the cookie completely.

4. Place the Crescent dough covered Tagalongs into the preheated and prepared Air Fryer basket and bake for 4-6 minutes, or until they are golden brown.
5. Remove from the Air Fryer basket and sprinkle with powdered sugar before serving.

NOTES

Each Air Fryer is different, so make sure to start checking your cookies for doneness within the last couple of minutes. I generally cook mine between 4-5 minutes, but I have seen others take a little longer to get golden brown.

Air Fryer Sausage

Servings: 6
Cooking Time: 8 Minutes

Ingredients:
- 6 thin Italian sausages Italian or standard
- 1 serving cooking spray

Directions:
1. Preheat the air fryer to 200C/400F.
2. Lightly pierce the sausages in 2 places, through their casing.
3. Lightly grease the air fryer basket, then add a single layer of sausages in it.
4. Air fry the sausage links for 8 minutes, or until fully cooked.

Notes

TO STORE: Pu leftovers in airtight containers to store in the refrigerator for 3-4 days.

TO FREEZE: Use freezer safe bags or containers to freeze sausages for up to 6 months.

TO REHEAT: Reheat in the microwave for a few seconds or in the air fryer for 2-3 minutes.

Air Fryer Pizza Recipe

Servings: 4-6
Cooking Time: 1 Hour 20 Minutes To 1 Hour 36 Minutes

Ingredients:
- 1 pound pizza dough, thawed if frozen
- Cooking spray
- 1 cup prepared pizza sauce
- 2 2/3 cups shredded Italian cheese blend
- TOPPING OPTIONS:
- Pepperoni
- Sliced mushrooms
- Sliced peppers

Directions:
1. Divide 1 pound pizza dough into 8 (2-ounce) pieces. If refrigerated, let sit on the counter until room temperature, at least 30 minutes.
2. Heat an air fryer to 375°F.
3. Press each piece of pizza dough into a round up to 6 1/2-inches wide, or 1/2 inch smaller than the size of your air fryer basket.
4. Coat the air fryer basket with cooking spray and carefully transfer one round of dough into the basket. (The basket will be warm.) Gently press the dough to the edges of the basket without touching the sides. Spread 2 tablespoons pizza sauce onto the dough, then sprinkle with 1/3 cup of the shredded cheese and top with any desired toppings.
5. Air fry until the crust is golden-brown and the cheese is melted, 10 to 12 minutes.
6. Carefully lift the pizza out of the air fryer basket with tongs or a spatula. Place on a cutting board and cut into wedges. Serve immediately and repeat with the remaining dough and toppings.

RECIPE NOTES

Storage: Leftovers can be refrigerated in an airtight container for up to 3 days.

Air Fryer Thin Mints

Servings: 4
Cooking Time: 5 Minutes

Ingredients:
- 4 crescent roll sheets
- 4 Thin Mints
- powdered sugar

Directions:
1. Preheat the air fryer to 360 degrees Fahrenheit and prepare the air fryer basket.

2. Open and separate the crescent roll dough into single crescent dough sheets.
3. Place a cookie at the wide end of the crescent dough sheet and then toll the dough to cover the entire cookie. Finish with the remainder of the cookies and crescent sheets.
4. Place the cookies onto a piece of parchment paper or prepared basket and then bake for 4-5 minutes, or until the dough is golden brown.
5. Carefully remove the Air Fryer Thin Mints and sprinkle with powdered sugar. Serve warm.

NOTES

You can use any of your favorite Girl Scouts cookies with this recipe.

Sprinkle the tops of the cookies with powdered sugar, and also drizzle them with dark chocolate or and of your favorite types of chocolate coating.

Frozen Potstickers In The Air Fryer

Servings: 2
Cooking Time: 10 Minutes

Ingredients:
- DUMPLINGS
- 8 ounces frozen vegetable, pork, or chicken dumplings
- DIPPING SAUCE
- 1/4 cup soy sauce
- 1/4 cup water
- 1/8 cup maple syrup (or molasses)
- 1/2 teaspoon garlic powder
- 1/2 teaspoon rice vinegar
- small pinch of red pepper flakes

Directions:
1. Preheat your air fryer to 370 degrees for about 4 minutes.
2. Place the frozen dumplings inside the air fryer in one layer and spray with oil.
3. Cook for 5 minutes, shake the basket, then spray with a little more oil.
4. Cook dumplings for another 4-6 minutes.

5. Meanwhile, prepare the dipping sauce by mixing ingredients together.
6. Remove the air fryer dumplings from the basket and let sit for another 2 minutes before enjoying.

Air Fryer Butternut Squash Soup

Servings: 4

Ingredients:
- Deselect All
- 1 1/2 pounds butternut squash (from about half of 1 large squash), peeled and cut into 1-inch pieces
- 2 medium carrots, cut into 1 1/2-inch pieces
- 1 orange bell pepper, stemmed, seeded and cut into 1-inch-thick slices
- 1/2 medium onion, cut into 4 wedges
- 3 tablespoons olive oil
- 3/4 teaspoon granulated garlic
- 1/2 teaspoon ground ginger
- 1/4 teaspoon dried thyme
- Kosher salt and freshly ground black pepper
- 3 cups low-sodium vegetable broth
- 1/2 cup heavy cream
- Roasted, salted pepitas, for serving
- Crème fraîche or full-fat plain yogurt, for serving
- Finely chopped chives, for serving

Directions:
1. Special equipment: a 6-quart air fryer
2. Preheat a 6-quart air fryer to 375 degrees F. Toss the butternut squash, carrots, bell pepper, onion, olive oil, granulated garlic, ginger, thyme, 1 1/2 teaspoons salt and several grinds of black pepper together in a large bowl until well combined. Transfer to the air fryer basket. Fry until golden brown and tender, tossing halfway through, about 20 minutes.
3. Transfer the browned vegetables to a large pot or Dutch oven and add the broth and cream. Use an immersion blender to blend the mixture on medium-high until very smooth. (Alternatively, blend the mixture

in a standard blender, first letting it cool for 5 minutes, then transferring it to the blender, filling only halfway. Put the lid on, leaving one corner open. Cover the lid with a kitchen towel to catch splatters, and pulse until very smooth, scrapping down the sides of the blender carafe with a rubber spatula as needed; pour the blended mixture back into the pot.)

4. Cook the soup over medium-low heat, stirring occasionally, until the mixture is just simmering, about 5 minutes. Taste and adjust the seasoning with salt and pepper. Ladle into bowls and top with pepitas, drizzle with crème fraîche or yogurt and sprinkle with chives.

Air Fryer Pierogies

Servings: 4
Cooking Time: 12 Minutes

Ingredients:
- 14 ounces pierogi frozen
- 1 tbsp olive oil
- Optional: Sour cream, carmelized onions, mushrooms, or your favorite dipping sauce.

Directions:
1. Evenly lay each piece flat in the basket of air fryer. Try to keep them from overlapping or stacking so they can cook more evenly while they are air frying.
2. Use cooking oil spray, brush olive oil, or toss to coat, covering both sides of each piece.
3. Once they are lightly coated with olive oil, cook at 400 degrees F for 10-12 minutes until they have a golden, crispy texture. Turn them over halfway through cooking.
4. Serve warm with sour cream, onions, mushrooms, or any of your favorite toppings.

Homemade Garlic Aioli

Servings: 8
Cooking Time: 0 Minutes

Ingredients:
- ½ cup mayonnaise
- 1 clove garlic minced
- 1 tablespoon lemon juice
- ¼ teaspoon kosher salt
- 2 teaspoons olive oil
- ¼ teaspoon pepper

Directions:
1. Mix all ingredients in a small bowl to combine.
2. Refrigerate at least 30 minutes before serving.

Notes
Makes approx 1 cup.
Keep in a tightly covered container in the fridge for about 2-3 days.

Air Fryer Fried Rice

Servings: 4
Cooking Time: 20 Minutes

Ingredients:
- 300g chicken tenderloins
- 4 rashers rindless bacon
- 450g packet microwave long-grain rice
- 2 tbsp oyster sauce
- 2 tbsp light soy sauce
- 1 tsp sesame oil
- 3 tsp finely grated fresh ginger
- 2 eggs, lightly whisked
- 120g (3/4 cup) frozen peas
- 2 green shallots, sliced
- 1 long fresh red chilli, thinly sliced
- Oyster sauce, to drizzle
- Select all ingredients

Directions:
1. Preheat the air fryer to 180C. Place the chicken and bacon on the air fryer rack. Cook for 8 minutes or until cooked through. Transfer to a plate and set aside to cool slightly. Slice the chicken and chop the bacon.

2. Meanwhile, use your fingers to separate the rice grains in the packet. Microwave the rice for 1 minute. Transfer to a round 20cm, high-sided ovenproof dish or cake pan. Add the oyster sauce, soy sauce, sesame oil, ginger and 2 tablespoons water. Stir to combine.

3. Place the dish or pan in the air fryer. Cook for 5 minutes or until the rice is tender. Stir through the egg, peas, chicken and half of the bacon. Cook for 3 minutes or until the egg is cooked through. Stir in half the shallot and season with salt and white pepper.

4. Serve sprinkled with chilli, remaining shallot, remaining bacon and extra oyster sauce.

3 Ingredient Dog Treats

Servings: 50
Cooking Time: 4 Hr

Ingredients:
- 2 cups rolled oats
- ½ cup peanut butter (only ingredient should be peanuts)
- ½ cup fruit or vegetable purée (apple, banana, sweet potato, or pumpkin are all great options)
- Items Needed
- Food processor
- Parchment paper
- Cookie cutters (optional)

Directions:
1. Place the oats in a food processor and blend until the oats turn into oat flour.
2. Add the peanut butter and fruit or vegetable purée of choice and blend until a dough forms.
3. Roll dough out to ¼-inch thickness between parchment paper so it doesn't stick.
4. Cut the dough out into 2-inch sized shapes using cookie cutters or a knife.
5. Place the treats evenly between the Food Dehydrator trays.

6. Set temperature to 145°F and time to 4 hours, then press Start/Stop.

7. Remove when done, cool to room temperature on the trays, then serve to your pet.

Lasagne Soup

Servings: 4-6
Cooking Time: 40 Minutes

Ingredients:
- 250g lasagne sheets broken in to medium sized pieces
- 500g beef mince
- 1 small red onion
- 2 crushed garlic cloves
- 1 tsp dried oregano
- 1 tsp dried basil
- 1 tsp dried thyme 1/4 cup tomato paste
- Olive oil to fry
- 1 1/2 cup canned diced tomatoes
- 1 tbsp sun dried tomato pesto
- 1 tbsp soy sauce
- 600ml liquid cream or coconut milk
- 4 cups vegetable stock (more if needed)
- Salt and pepper to taste
- Fried bacon for topping
- Fried halloumi for topping
- Fresh herbs for topping
- Fresh bread

Directions:
1. Heat your Vortex Oven on Bake to 170 degrees Celsius.
2. Add a generous dollop of olive oil to your baking dish of choice, add in the diced onion, garlic and the herbs and place in the oven to caramelise a bit.
3. Quickly remove, stir and add in the meat, place back in the oven and let it cook for 5 minutes before removing again to stir, add in a bit of salt to taste, and then add in the rest or the soup ingredients, and half of the lasagne noodles. Let it cook for 10 minutes, making sure the noodles are covered.
4. After 10 minutes add the rest of the noodles, stir, if you like and then add the cream or

coconut milk, let it cook for 25-30 minutes stirring every now and again to make sure the noodles dont stick together.

5. While the soup is bubbling away, place the bacon and halloumi in a baking dish, drizzle with olive oil and place on the bottom rack of the vortex oven to crisp up.

6. Switch the baking to grill for 5-8 minutes. When the noodles are soft, taste to see if you need to add more salt, serve the soup with crispy bacon and fried halloumi, fresh herbs, more cream and crispy bread on the side.

Air Fryer Deep-dish Pepperoni Pizza

Servings: 4

Ingredients:
- 1 can (13.8 oz) refrigerated Pillsbury™ Classic Crust Pizza Crust
- 1 tablespoon olive oil
- 1/3 cup pizza sauce
- 1 cup shredded mozzarella cheese (4 oz)
- 11 pepperoni slices (0.8 oz)
- 2 tablespoons shredded Parmesan cheese

Directions:
1. Cut 8-inch round of cooking parchment paper. Place in bottom of air fryer basket. Spray with cooking spray. Unroll dough, and tuck corners under. Shape into 10-inch round with thicker 1-inch border.
2. Press into air fryer basket on top of parchment. Press 1 1/2 inches up side of basket.
3. Set to 325°F; cook 10 minutes. Turn pizza crust over on counter; remove parchment, and replace in air fryer basket. Cool 2 to 3 minutes or until cool enough to handle.
4. Using fingers, press center of crust down, making 1-inch border. Brush sides and top of crust all over with olive oil. Place in basket. Cook 5 minutes longer.
5. Top center of dough with pizza sauce. Top with mozzarella cheese, then top with pepperoni, followed by Parmesan cheese.

Cook 4 to 7 minutes longer or until cooked through and cheese is melted. Cool 2 minutes. Remove from basket with rubber spatula.

Crispy Peanut Tofu With Squash Noodles

Servings: 4
Cooking Time: 20 Minutes

Ingredients:
- FOR THE PEANUT SAUCE:
- 6 tablespoons powdered peanut butter I like PB2
- 1 clove garlic small, finely grated
- 1/2 teaspoon ginger paste
- 1 tablespoon low-sodium tamari or low-sodium soy sauce
- 1 teaspoon toasted sesame oil
- 1/2 teaspoon Chinese cooking wine
- FOR THE PEANUT TOFU AND SQUASH NOODLES:
- 14 ounces extra firm tofu drained, pressed and diced into cubes
- 2 tablespoons low-sodium tamari or low-sodium soy sauce
- 1 teaspoon toasted sesame oil
- 1 tablespoon cornstarch
- 2 teaspoons toasted sesame seeds optional
- olive oil spray
- 2 medium yellow squash spiralized
- 2 medium zucchinis spiralized
- 6 to 8 ounces shiitake mushrooms stems removed and caps sliced
- 1/4 teaspoon garlic powder
- FOR SERVING:
- 1/4 cup chopped peanuts for serving
- cilantro chopped, for serving
- 2 green onions sliced, for serving
- sambal oelek for serving
- lime wedges for serving
- sesame seeds for serving

Directions:
1. FOR THE SAUCE:

2. In a small bowl, combine the powdered peanut butter with 3 tablespoons of water, mixing until combined.
3. Next stir in the garlic, ginger, tamari, toasted sesame oil and Chinese cooking wine.
4. When ready to serve, heat in a small sauce pan until warmed
5. FOR THE TOFU AND SQUASH NOODLES:
6. Cut the (pressed) tofu into ½-inch cubes.
7. In a medium bowl, combine 2 tablespoons tamari, 1 teaspoon sesame oil and cornstarch. Once combined, toss with sesame seeds.
8. Then, preheat your air fryer to 390° or 400° depending on your model. Working in batches, add the tofu in a single layer and air fry for 8 to 10 minutes or until crispy. Transfer to a paper towel lined plate and repeat with the remaining tofu.
9. Then add the sliced shiitake into the air fryer and cook for 4 minutes. You can reheat the tofu by adding it back into your air fryer and heating for a minute or two.
10. FOR THE SQUASH NOODLES:
11. Heat a 10-inch skillet over medium heat and spray with olive oil spray.
12. Once hot, add the spiralized squash noodles and the garlic powder. Toss occasionally until tender yet still a bit firm. About 7 to 8 minutes.
13. Finally serve the zoodles into bowls and add the crispy tofu, shiitake mushrooms and peanut sauce. Then top with crushed peanuts, sliced green onions, sesame seeds and minced cilantro. Don't forget about the wedge of lime on the side.

Air Fryer Italian Sausage

Servings: 2
Cooking Time: 11 Minutes

Ingredients:
- 2 sausages
- bun optional for serving

Directions:

1. Preheat the air fryer to 360°F.
2. Spread the sausage out in a single layer in the air fryer basket.
3. Cook for 5 minutes, then flip the sausage and cook an additional 5-6 minutes or until cooked through.

Notes

Preheat the air fryer for best results.

Do not poke the sausage before cooking, this will release all of the fats that keep sausages juicy.

Sausages can be sliced before air frying. More of the fats will drain this way.

Place parchment paper on the bottom of the air fryer tray when you add the sausage (never preheat with parchment paper) or basket for a quick and easy clean-up!

Air Fryer Biscuit Dough Pizzas

Servings: 8
Cooking Time: 10 Minutes

Ingredients:
- 1 can Grands! refrigerated biscuits (8 biscuits)
- 1 cup (240 ml) pizza sauce or tomato sauce
- 1 cup (113 g) shredded cheese
- salt , to taste
- black pepper , to taste
- OPTIONAL TOPPINGS
- Pepperoni, cooked Sausage, Bacon pieces, diced Ham, sliced or diced Tomatoes, Mushrooms, Pineapple, etc.
- OTHER SAUCE OPTIONS
- BBQ Sauce, Salsa, White (Alfredo) Sauce, Pesto, etc.
- EQUIPMENT
- Air Fryer
- Air Fryer Rack optional

Directions:
1. Separate the biscuits, then flatten and roll out each biscuit to 5-inches (13cm) wide.
2. Place in the air fryer basket/tray in a single layer (cook in batches if needed - do not top with sauce or toppings yet).

3. Air Fry at 330°F/166°C for 3 minutes. Flip the biscuit dough over. Continue to Air Fry at 330°F/166°C for another 3-4 minutes, or until cooked through.
4. Spread about 2 Tablespoons of sauce over each biscuit dough base. Then sprinkle about 2 Tablespoons of cheese on top. Add additional salt, pepper and other desired toppings.
5. Place the biscuit dough pizzas in the air fryer basket/tray in a single layer (cook in batches if needed). To keep your topping from flying around, place an air fryer rack over the pizzas.
6. Increase the heat and Air Fry the pizzas at 360°F/182°C for 2-5 minutes or until heated through and cheese is melted.

Air Fryer Frozen Pizza

Servings: 1
Cooking Time: 6 Minutes

Ingredients:
- 1 personal frozen pizza

Directions:
1. Preheat your air fryer to 350 degrees.
2. Place the frozen pizza in the air fryer and cook for 6 to 8 minutes* until pizza is hot and cheese is melted.
3. Remove the pizza from the air fryer and enjoy!

NOTES

*If cooking frozen French bread pizza or Ellio's frozen pizza, cook at 400 degrees for about 5 minutes.

HOW TO REHEAT MINI PIZZA IN THE AIR FRYER:

Preheat your air fryer to 350 degrees.

Cook the pizza for 2 to 3 minutes until warmed then enjoy!

Dutch Baby

Servings: 3

Ingredients:
- 3 extra-large eggs, room temperature
- ½ cup all-purpose flour, sifted
- ½ cup whole milk, room temperature
- 1 tablespoon granulated sugar
- 1 teaspoon ground nutmeg
- 2½ tablespoons unsalted butter
- ½ lemon, juiced, for sprinkling (optional)
- Confectioner's sugar, for dusting
- Fresh berries, for garnish (optional)
- Items Needed:
- 7-inch cast iron pan or 7-inch cake pan
- Metal sieve
- Oven mitt or kitchen towels

Directions:
1. Place the cast iron pan or cake pan into the Air Fryer basket.
2. Select the Preheat function on the air fryer, adjust temperature to 375°F, then press Start/Pause.
3. Whisk the eggs, flour, milk, sugar, and nutmeg in a large bowl until well combined and smooth. There should be no lumps.
4. Remove the air fryer basket after preheating, keeping the cast iron pan inside the basket. Immediately add in the butter and use a spatula to spread the butter around evenly until it has melted.
5. Pour the batter into the cast iron pan and reinsert the basket back into the air fryer.
6. Set temperature to 375°F and time to 20 minutes, then press Start/Pause. The pancake will puff up and grow in height, no shake is necessary but if you would like a lighter colored topping, pause the air fryer when 5 minutes is left on the timer and tent the top of the pancake with foil.
7. Remove the cast iron pan, carefully with an oven mitt, when done. Turn out the Dutch baby onto a serving platter and serve at once sprinkled with lemon juice, dusted with confectioner's sugar, and fresh berries if desired.

Air Fryer Hot Dogs

Servings: 4
Cooking Time: 5 Minutes

Ingredients:
- 4 Hot Dogs
- 4 Hot Dog Buns

Directions:
1. Take the hot dogs out of packaging, then cut a diagonal slits into each hot dog.
2. Place hot dogs in air fryer in a single layer. Air fry at 400 degrees F for 5-7 minutes cooking time.
3. Once hot dogs are done, use tongs or a fork to remove from the basket. Place hot dogs in bun, then place buns into air fryer basket.
4. Return hotdogs and buns to air fryer and air fry again at 400 degrees F for 1-2 minutes, until bun is a golden color.
5. Remove from air fryer basket and serve with favorite delicious toppings, such as ketchup, mustard, or BBQ sauce.

Air Fryer Frozen Mozzarella Sticks

Servings: 24
Cooking Time: 6 Minutes

Ingredients:
- 24 Frozen mozzarella sticks or bites this can be any brand of choice

Directions:
1. Preheat the air fryer at 180C/360F for 3 minutes.
2. Remove the frozen mozzarella sticks from its packaging and carefully arrange it in the preheated air fryer basket in a single layer making sure to leave some spaces in between them
3. Cook at 180C/360F for 6 minutes or until crispy on the outside and cheese melted in the middle.
4. Serve immediately with marinara dipping sauce or pizza sauce. enjoy!
NOTES

PS: most recipe websites suggest cooking at 200C/400F, personally, I believe this would only cook the mozzarella sticks too quickly and explode during cooking.
Tips
I used Cosori 5.7l air fryer and was able to fit 24 frozen cheese pieces in the basket. If you are catering for more then be sure to cook them in batches.
Do not thaw before cooking and avoid stacking them so that they cook evenly Flip the cheese sticks halfway through the cooking time if need be, I did not need to do this
No need to spray the air fry basket with cooking oil for this recipe

Air Fryer Stuffed Jalapenos

Servings: 2
Cooking Time: 7 Minutes

Ingredients:
- 3 jalapenos cut in half lengthwise and deseeded
- ¼ cup cream cheese softened
- ¼ cup nacho cheese mix shredded
- 1 tablespoon bacon bits
- 1 green onion sliced

Directions:
1. Preheat the air fryer to 350°F.
2. Cut the jalapenos lengthwise and remove the seeds
3. In a small bowl combine the remaining ingredients and mix until combined.
4. Fill each jalapeno with the cheese mixture and place in the air fryer basket.
5. Cook jalapenos for 5-7 minutes or until the peppers are tender and cheese has browned on top.
Notes
If you want to cook larger amounts, simply double or triple. If you try to do more than one rack at a time, you will need to rotate them and make sure to not put any racks higher than the middle rung, they will get scorched on the top!

SNACKS & APPETIZERS RECIPES

Air Fryer Sweet Potato Fries

Servings: 2
Cooking Time: 12 Minutes

Ingredients:

- 2 medium sweet potatoes peeled
- 2 teaspoons olive oil
- ½ teaspoon salt
- ¼ teaspoon garlic powder
- ¼ teaspoon paprika
- ⅛ teaspoon black pepper

Directions:

1. Preheat the air fryer to 380°F. Peel the sweet potatoes, then slice each potato into even 1/4 inch thick sticks.
2. Place the sweet potatoes in a large mixing bowl, and toss with olive oil, salt, garlic powder, paprika and black pepper.
3. Cook in 2 or 3 batches, depending on the size of your basket without overcrowding the pan until they're crispy. I recommend 12 minutes, turning half way. This may vary based on your air fryer.
4. Serve immediately with your favorite dipping sauce.

Notes

Storage: Store any leftovers in an airtight container. They will last about 3-4 days in the fridge. To reheat, just place in the air fryer at 360°F for 1-2 minutes or in a toaster oven. You can also reheat in the microwave but the potatoes will be soft if heated in the microwave.
Substitutes: For best results, follow the recipe as is. However you can switch out the spices and use a different oil
Equipment: I used the NuWave Air Fryer to make this recipe. It's easy to use with guides on the appliance, easy to clean up and I've been very happy with the results!

Air Fryer Frozen Onion Rings

Servings: 4
Cooking Time: 20 Minutes

Ingredients:

- 1- 14 ounce bag frozen onion rings
- non-stick cooking spray

Directions:

1. Layer half of the bag of frozen onion rings into the basket of the air fryer. Make sure to layer them in one layer making sure not to overlap the onion rings.
2. Lightly spray the onion rings with non-stick cooking spray. This gives them extra crispiness.
3. Close the air fryer and cook at 400 degrees Fahrenheit for 8-10 minutes.
4. Halfway through the cooking process, open the basket and flip the onion rings. Continue to cook to desired crispness.
5. Remove the cooked onion rings from the basket and repeat these steps for the remaining frozen onion rings.
6. Enjoy right away with your favorite dipping sauce!

Air Fryer Zucchini Chips

Servings: 4
Cooking Time: 8 Minutes

Ingredients:

- 1 medium-sized zucchini
- 1/2 cup panko breadcrumbs
- 1/2 teaspoon garlic powder
- 1/4 teaspoon onion powder
- 1 egg
- 3 tablespoons flour

Directions:

1. Cut zucchini into thin slices, approximately 1/4 inches.
2. Mix panko breadcrumbs, garlic powder, and onion powder in a bowl.
3. Whisk one egg into a separate bowl and put the flour in a third bowl.

4. Dip zucchini into the flour, then the egg, then the breadcrumbs.
5. Place the breaded zucchini in an air fryer in a single layer and cook at 380 degrees for 7-9 minutes, flipping halfway.
6. Enjoy immediately.

Air Fryer Roasted Butternut Squash & Kale Salad With Balsamic-maple Dressing

Servings: 4-6

Ingredients:
- 1 medium butternut squash (about 2 lb.), peeled, seeded, and cut into 1" pieces (about 6 c.)
- 2 tbsp. plus 2 tsp. extra-virgin olive oil
- 1 tsp. kosher salt, divided, plus more
- 1/4 tsp. freshly ground black pepper
- 2 tbsp. balsamic vinegar
- 2 tsp. maple syrup
- 1 tsp. Dijon mustard
- 1 bunch of curly kale, stems removed, leaves roughly chopped (about 6 packed c.)
- 1/4 c. dried cranberries
- 2 tbsp. raw pumpkin seeds (pepitas)
- 2 oz. goat cheese

Directions:
1. In a large bowl, toss squash, 2 teaspoons oil, 1/2 teaspoon salt, and 1/4 teaspoon pepper. Scrape into an air-fryer basket; reserve bowl. Cook at 400°, shaking basket or tossing squash a few times, until squash is tender and golden, about 15 minutes.
2. Meanwhile, in reserved bowl, whisk vinegar, syrup, mustard, 1/2 teaspoon salt, and remaining 2 tbsp. oil. Add kale and massage into dressing to soften a bit.
3. Transfer squash to bowl with kale. Add cranberries and pepitas and toss to combine; season with salt and pepper. Crumble goat cheese over and gently toss into salad.

Air Fryer Crunchy Chili-spiced Chickpeas

Servings: 2-4

Ingredients:
- 1 (15-oz.) can chickpeas, rinsed and drained
- 1 tbsp. extra-virgin olive oil
- 2 tsp. chili powder
- 1/4 tsp. kosher salt
- Finely grated lime zest, for serving

Directions:
1. Dry chickpeas very well with paper towels. In a medium bowl, toss chickpeas, oil, chili powder, and salt.
2. Transfer chickpea mixture to an air-fryer basket, scraping bowl to get all of the oil. Cook at 370° until crispy and golden brown, 10 to 14 minutes.
3. Serve chickpeas warm or at room temperature. Grate lime zest over top.

Air Fryer Avocado Fries

Servings: 4
Cooking Time: 8 Minutes

Ingredients:
- 2 large avocados sliced
- 1 cup panko breadcrumbs
- 1/2 cup Italian breadcrumbs
- 1/4 cup all purpose flour
- 1 egg beaten
- 1/2 teaspoon ground black pepper
- 1/2 teaspoon garlic powder
- 1/4 teaspoon sea salt
- 1 teaspoon avocado spray

Directions:
1. Preheat the air fryer to 370 degrees Fahrenheit.
2. Add the Italian breadcrumbs, flour, black pepper, garlic powder, and sea salt into a rimmed dish.
3. Add the panko breadcrumbs to a rimmed dish.
4. Add the beaten egg to a small bowl.

5. Create a dipping station by setting each dish next to each other in an assembly line type setup.
6. Begin by rolling an avocado slice in the flour, tapping to remove any excess flour from the slice. Take the flour dipped avocado slice and place it into the egg mixture, then dip into the breadcrumbs mixture, and finally the panko breadcrumbs last.
7. Repeat the process with all of the remaining avocado slices.
8. Prepare the air fryer basket with avocado oil spray.
9. Carefully line the breaded avocados in a single layer in the air fryer basket. Make sure to leave room in between each slice to allow for complete air circulation.
10. Spray the avocado slices with a light coat of avocado oil, and then air fry at 370 degrees Fahrenheit for 7-8 minutes, flipping them halfway through.
11. Serve with your favorite dipping sauce.

NOTES

All air fryers cook a little differently. This recipe was made using a 5.8 qt basket style Cosori air fryer. If you are using a different brand of air fryer, make sure you do a "test run" of this recipe to see if you need to adjust the cooking time.

Dipping sauces are a great way to add different flavors to this recipe. I think that ranch dressing, BBQ sauce, or even your favorite hot sauce or spicy sauce are the perfect flavor enhancers.

Add a little bit of parmesan cheese into the panko mixture for simple salty addition.

Squeeze a little bit of lime juice over the top of the avocados after they're cooked in the air fryer. This gives a tasty citrus flavor! (Lemon juice works well, too!)

Air-fryer Pickle Chips

Servings: 6

Ingredients:
- 2 cup sliced dill pickles
- 3 tablespoon cornstarch
- ½ teaspoon salt
- ¼ teaspoon black pepper
- ½ cup buttermilk
- 2 tablespoon Sriracha sauce
- 1 ¼ cup panko bread crumbs
- 1 tablespoon vegetable oil
- ½ cup ranch salad dressing

Directions:
1. Preheat air-fryer to 400°F. Lay pickle slices on a paper-towel lined baking sheet; pat dry.
2. In a shallow dish combine cornstarch, salt, and pepper. In another shallow dish combine buttermilk and 1 Tbsp. Sriracha. In a third shallow dish combine panko and oil.
3. Working in batches, gently coat dried pickle slices in cornstarch mixture, shaking off excess, then coat in buttermilk mixture. Roll in panko to coat.
4. Place breaded pickle slices in basket (do not overcrowd). Cook for 6 to 8 minutes or until golden brown. Keep cooked slices in a 200°F oven while cooking the remaining slices.
5. Meanwhile, in a small bowl combine ranch dressing and remaining 1 Tbsp. Sriracha.
6. Serve pickle chips immediately with spicy ranch.

Air Fryer French Fries

Servings: 4
Cooking Time: 20 Minutes

Ingredients:
- 2 medium sized russet potatoes
- 1 tablespoon olive oil
- 1 teaspoon Italian seasoning
- 2 tablespoons Parmesan cheese, grated
- 1/2 teaspoon salt
- 1/4 teaspoon pepper

Directions:
1. Preheat the air fryer to 380 degrees Fahrenheit. Slice the potatoes using a fry cutter, or slice them into 1/4-inch strips.

2. Rinse the potato slices in cold water and pat dry with a paper towel.
3. In a medium-sized bowl toss with olive oil, Italian seasoning, Parmesan cheese, salt, and pepper.
4. Place the fries into the basket of the air fryer in a single layer. Cook for 15-20 minutes or until golden brown.
5. Toss the fries halfway through the cooking process to ensure the fries get evenly cooked.
6. Serve with ketchup or fry sauce.

Air Fryer Frozen Waffle Fries

Servings: 4
Cooking Time: 20 Minutes

Ingredients:

- 16 ounces Frozen Waffle Fries
- Olive Oil Spray
- Salt or seasoning salt to Taste

Directions:

1. Place the frozen fries in the basket of your air fryer and spray lightly with olive oil spray.
2. Cook at 400°F degrees for 10 minutes. Shake the fries and cook for an additional 5-10 minutes until crispy.
3. Season with salt or seasoned salt if needed!

Air Fryer Green Beans

Servings: 4
Cooking Time: 6 Minutes

Ingredients:

- 1 lb green beans trimmed
- 2 tablespoons olive oil
- 1/2 teaspoon salt
- 1/2 teaspoon pepper

Directions:

1. Preheat the air fryer to 190C/375F.
2. In a mixing bowl, add the trimmed beans then toss through the olive oil, salt, and pepper.

3. Add a single layer of the beans to the air fryer basket and air fry for 8 minutes, shaking halfway through. Repeat the process until all the beans are cooked.
4. Sprinkle with parmesan cheese and add a squeeze of lemon juice.

Notes

TO STORE: Leftovers can be stored in the refrigerator, covered, for up to 5 days.

TO FREEZE: Place the cooked and cooled beans in a ziplock bag and store them in the freezer for up to 6 months.

TO REHEAT: Either microwave for a few seconds or reheat in the air fryer for 1-2 minutes.

Air Fryer Kale Chips

Servings: 4
Cooking Time: 5 Minutes

Ingredients:

- BASIC AIR FRYER KALE CHIPS:
- 1 lb Curly Kale
- 1 tbsp Olive oil
- 1/2 tsp Sea salt
- LEMON GARLIC:
- 2 tbsp Lemon juice
- 2 tsp Lemon zest
- 1 tsp Garlic powder
- CHILI LIME:
- 4 tsp Lime juice
- 2 tsp Chili powder
- 1/2 tsp Garlic powder
- TACO:
- 4 tsp Taco Seasoning
- RANCH:
- 4 tsp Ranch seasoning
- BBQ:
- 3 tbsp BBQ sauce
- CAJUN:
- 1 tbsp Cajun seasoning
- SALT AND VINEGAR:
- 3 tbsp White vinegar
- NACHO CHEESE:
- 3 tbsp Cheddar cheese powder
- 1/4 tsp Cumin
- 1/4 tsp Garlic powder

- 1/4 tsp Onion powder
- 1/2 tsp Chili powder
- 1/4 tsp Paprika
- FLAMIN' HOT:
- 2 tbsp Cheddar cheese powder
- 2-3 tbsp Hot sauce
- 1/2 tsp Garlic powder
- SOUR CREAM AND ONION:
- 2 tbsp Buttermilk powder
- 1/2 tbsp Onion powder
- 2 tsp Dried parsley

Directions:

1. Wash kale and dry thoroughly. (Kale chips will take longer to crisp up if you don't dry the kale well).
2. Use a sharp knife to slice around the tough stem of each kale leaf. Discard stem. Roughly chop kale into bite-sized pieces.
3. Place kale in a large mixing bowl. Add the olive oil and salt. If making flavored kale chips, add the other ingredients as well, in addition to the basic kale chips ingredients. Toss, using your hands to gently massage the kale to make sure each leaf is well coated.
4. Preheat air fryer to 325 degrees F (163 degrees C).
5. Place kale in the air fryer basket. (You can cook in 2 batches if it doesn't all fit.) Cook for 3 minutes, then shake the basket and cook for another 2-3 minutes, until the air fryer kale chips are crispy and dried out.
6. For lemon garlic, chili lime, or salt and vinegar, or flamin' hot kale chips, add an extra 1-2 minutes. For BBQ kale chips, add an extra 3-4 minutes.

Air Fryer Pasta Chips

Servings: 4
Cooking Time: 20 Minutes

Ingredients:

- 8 oz. (227 g) dried Bowtie (Farfalle) Pasta, or pasta shape of choice
- 1 Tablespoon (15 ml) Olive Oil or Vegetable Oil

- 1 teaspoon (5 ml) Garlic Powder
- 1/3 cup (35 g) Parmesan Cheese
- 1/2 teaspoon (2.5 ml) Kosher Salt , or to taste
- Optional - additional seasonings of choice - Italian seasoning , dried basil, onion powder, etc.
- EQUIPMENT
- Air Fryer

Directions:

1. In a large pot of salted boiling water, cook the pasta to package directions. Cook until it is tender (it crisps up best if it is cooked a little beyond al dente).
2. Drain the pasta and put in a bowl. Toss with the olive oil, garlic powder, parmesan cheese, and salt (it should be well seasoned).
3. Cooking in batches if needed, put just a single layer of the seasoned pasta in the air fryer basket/tray. (For most air fryers, cook in batches to avoid overcrowding the basket/tray. For best results air fry in just a single layer.)
4. Air Fry at 380°F/195°C for 7-10 minutes, shaking and stirring the pasta every 2-3 minutes making sure to separate any pasta sticking together. (Shaking often helps them crispy evenly and not burnt.) Cook until the pasta is golden and crispy to your liking. Timing will vary depending on your air fryer model, type of pasta you're cooking and preferred texture.
5. If cooking in batches, the next batches might cook quicker because the air fryer is already hot. Serve with warmed marinara sauce or sauce of choice.

Air Fryer Frozen French Fries

Servings: 4
Cooking Time: 15 Minutes

Ingredients:

- 1 pound (454 g) frozen french fries
- Kosher salt or sea salt , to taste
- ground black pepper , to taste optional
- EQUIPMENT

- Air Fryer

Directions:
1. Place the frozen fries in air fryer basket and spread them evenly over the basket. You don't need to spray extra oil.
2. Air fry the frozen fries at 400°F/205°C for about 15 minutes (about 10 minutes for thin cut fries). About halfway through cooking, shake the basket and gently turn the fries. Try not to break them. For crisper, evenly cooked fries, turn them multiples times while cooking.
3. Air Fry for additional 1-3 minutes to crisp to your preferred liking. Season with salt and pepper if desired.

NOTES

No Oil Necessary. Cook Fries Frozen - Do not thaw first.

Shake several times for even cooking & Don't overcrowd fryer basket.

If cooking in multiple batches, the first batch will take longer to cook if Air Fryer is not already pre-heated.

Recipes were cooked in 3-4 qt air fryers. If using a larger air fryer, the recipe might require more time.

Remember to set a timer to shake/flip/toss the food as directed in recipe.

Air Fryer Home Fries

Servings: 4
Cooking Time: 20 Minutes

Ingredients:
- 1 1/2 pounds russet potatoes
- 2 Tablespoons olive oil
- 1/4 cup onion chopped
- 1/3 cup bell pepper red, chopped
- 1 teaspoon garlic salt
- 1 teaspoon paprika
- 1/2 teaspoon ground black pepper

Directions:
1. Peel and rinse potatoes in cold water to remove excess starch.
2. Then cut them into 1-inch cubes.

3. Lay them out on a cutting board covered with a paper towel or a clean towel to absorb excess moisture.
4. Combine in a medium bowl the olive oil, red bell pepper and chopped onion.
5. Next add the garlic salt, paprika and black pepper into the mixing bowl.
6. Toss all the ingredients together until fully coated.
7. Place the seasoned home fries into the air fryer basket in a single layer allowing adequate space so they cook evenly.
8. Cook at 400 degrees F for 20 minutes. Shaking the basket halfway through the air frying cooking process.
9. Potatoes will be crispy and golden brown when done.
10. Serve immediately while hot.

NOTES

I make this recipe in my Cosori 5.8-quart air fryer. Depending on your type of air fryer, size and wattages, cook time may need to be adjusted an additional minute or two.

Because these fries go with almost any sauce, it's really a taste preference. I love spicy chipotle sauce, ranch dressing, tangy western sauce, blue cheese dressing, creamy cheese sauce, or with the original sauce ketchup.

I love topping these fries with a bit of parmesan cheese, salsa, chili, shredded cheeses, sour cream or hot sauce.

Air Fryer Carrot Fries

Servings: 2-3
Cooking Time: 14 Minutes

Ingredients:
- 4-5 carrots, peeled
- 2 teaspoon cornstarch
- ½ teaspoon parsley
- ½ teaspoon garlic powder
- ¼ teaspoon salt
- 1 tablespoon olive oil
- ½ tablespoon grated parmesan

Directions:
1. Preheat your air fryer to 400 degrees F.

2. Peel your carrots. Cut each carrot in half to make shorter fries. Then cut them lengthwise in half and then half them again lengthwise. They should all be about the same size for even cooking.
3. In a small bowl combine the cornstarch, parsley, garlic powder, and salt. Place your carrots in a dish and drizzle your olive oil over them. Next, sprinkle the seasoning over the carrots, mixing them till they are coated evenly.
4. Place them in a single layer in your air fryer basket. Cook for 13 to 15 minutes. They should be fork tender but hold their shape when held up. Let them rest for just a few minutes, allowing them to crisp up a little bit more. Place them on a plate and sprinkle with parmesan cheese. Serve immediately.

NOTES
HOW TO REHEAT CARROT FRIES IN THE AIR FRYER
Preheat the air fryer to 350 degrees F.
Lay the leftover carrot fries in a single layer in the air fryer basket.
Cook for 3 to 4 minutes until heated through.

Crispy Air Fryer French Fries

Servings: 3-4
Cooking Time: 12 Minutes

Ingredients:
- 2 medium russet potatoes, scrubbed
- 1 tablespoon olive oil
- 1/4 teaspoon salt
- 1/4 teaspoon garlic powder (optional)
- pinch of black pepper, to taste
- flaked sea salt, for serving

Directions:
1. Preheat the air fryer on 375 F for 5 minutes.
2. Slice the potatoes into long strips (french fry shape), roughly 1/4-inch thick. (I keep the skin on but you can peel the skin if you prefer).

3. Transfer sliced potatoes into a large bowl and add olive oil, salt, garlic powder (optional), and pepper. Toss to coat.
4. Place a single layer of potatoes into the air fryer basket and cook for 12-13 minutes, until crispy and golden. Do not overlap the potatoes as they will not cook evenly and crispy. I usually have to do this in 2 batches for the size of my air fryer.
5. Serve immediately with some flaked sea salt on top and a side of ketchup, spicy mayo or other dipping sauce.

NOTES
Equipment used: I used the Philips Digital Turbostar Air Fryer. We love it and have only good things to say about it.
How to double the recipe: You can double or triple the recipe, but you will have to make it in batches. To get tender but crispy french fries, you need to place them in the air fryer basket in one layer. If you start stacking them up and overcrowding the basket, they will not cook evenly and you may not get that crispy texture.
How to bake in the oven: To bake in the oven instead, spread the fries in an even layer on a large baking sheet. Bake for 25-30 minutes at 425 F, flipping the fries over halfway.

Air Fryer Garlic Parmesan French Fries

Servings: 6
Cooking Time: 18 Minutes

Ingredients:
- 4 large Yukon Gold potatoes
- 1 tablespoon olive oil
- 1 teaspoon kosher salt
- ¼ cup parmesan cheese, finely grated
- ½ teaspoon garlic powder
- 1 teaspoon parsley

Directions:
1. Rinse and scrub the potatoes under cold water.
2. Using a sharp knife, cut potatoes into thin 1/4 inch strips.

3. Transfer the potato strips to a large bowl, cover with ice water, and let the potatoes soak for about 30 minutes.
4. Drain the water and pat the potatoes dry.
5. Add oil and salt to the bowl and toss to coat.
6. Working in batches, place potatoes into a greased air fryer basket in a single layer. (Try not to overlap.)
7. Air fry at 380°F for 18-20 minutes, turning once halfway through.
8. While the fries are cooking, mix together the parmesan cheese, garlic powder, and parsley in a small bowl.
9. Remove the fries from the air fryer and toss them with the parmesan, garlic powder, and parsley mixture. Serve immediately.

Air Fryer Flower Fries

Servings: 12

Ingredients:
- Deselect All
- 12 small yellow potatoes, such as baby gold (about 1 pound)
- Olive oil spray
- 1 teaspoon kosher salt
- 6 teaspoons ranch dressing, plus more for serving
- 6 red and yellow cherry tomatoes, halved
- Baby arugula, for serving

Directions:
1. Special equipment: a 16-slice thin apple slicer, a melon baller, a 6-quart air fryer
2. Line up the potatoes and slice one end from each, taking off more or less to ensure that all the potatoes are the same length. (Reserve all the potato scraps: you can toss them with salt and oil to air fry later.)
3. Stand up each potato on its flat side. Working with 1 potato at a time, place a 16-slice thin apple slicer over the center of the rounded end. Carefully push the slicer down using a see-sawing motion until the blades are 1/4 inch from the bottom of the potato. Don't push firmly straight down or you could accidentally slice through the

entire potato. Remove the slicer by grasping the sides with both hands and firmly pushing your thumbs into the center of the potato. Use a melon baller to scoop out three-fourths of that center.
4. Thoroughly coat the potatoes all over with olive oil spray and season with the salt. Add them flat-sides down to a 6-quart air fryer. Cook at 380 degrees F until the petals are crispy and golden brown, 14 to 17 minutes depending on the size of your potatoes (see Cook's Note). Remove the air fryer basket, wait until the potatoes are cool enough to handle (about 1 minute) and gently pluck them out of the basket with your hands. Fill each center with 1/2 teaspoon ranch dressing and nestle half a cherry tomato on top, dome-side up. Arrange the potato flowers on a bed of baby arugula and serve with more ranch for dipping.

Cook's Note

Settings may vary on your air fryer depending on the model. Please refer to the manufacturer's guide.

Air Fryer Fried Pickles

Servings: 6

Ingredients:
- Deselect All
- Pickles:
- One 16-ounce jar dill pickle chips
- 1/2 cup all-purpose flour
- 1/4 teaspoon ground cayenne pepper
- 1 1/2 teaspoons Cajun seasoning
- 1 cup buttermilk
- A couple of dashes hot sauce
- 1 1/2 cups panko
- 1 teaspoon Italian seasoning
- Kosher salt
- 1 tablespoon olive oil
- Dipping sauce:
- 1/2 cup mayonnaise
- 4 teaspoons ketchup
- 1 teaspoon prepared horseradish
- 1/2 teaspoon Cajun seasoning

Directions:

1. For the pickles: Preheat a 3.5-quart air fryer to 390 degrees F. Set a wire rack inside a baking sheet.
2. Drain the pickles and spread them out on a paper towel-lined baking sheet. Pat dry with more paper towels, pressing gently to remove as much moisture as possible. Eliminate any pickles with large holes or ones that are very thin.
3. Set up a breading station using 3 medium bowls: Whisk together the flour, cayenne and 1/2 teaspoon Cajun seasoning in one bowl. In the second bowl combine the buttermilk and hot sauce. In the last combine the panko, Italian seasoning, the remaining 1 teaspoon Cajun seasoning and 1/2 teaspoon salt. Drizzle in the oil and use your hands to toss and coat the panko.
4. Working in small batches, bread the pickles: First, toss a handful of pickles in the flour mixture, shaking off any excess. Then dunk them in the buttermilk mixture to completely coat, shaking to remove any excess. Finally, toss them in the panko, pressing gently to make it adhere. Arrange the breaded pickles on the prepared baking sheet and repeat until all the pickles are breaded.
5. Arrange one-third of the breaded pickles in the basket of the air fryer in a single layer. Cook for 8 minutes, the pickles will be very crunchy and browned on both sides. Remove to a serving plate and repeat with the remaining two batches of pickles.
6. For the dipping sauce: Meanwhile, whisk together the mayonnaise, ketchup, horseradish and Cajun seasoning in small bowl.
7. Serve the warm pickles with the dipping sauce or use them and the dipping sauce to top your favorite burger.

Easy Air Fryer Green Beans

Servings: 4
Cooking Time: 6 Minutes

Ingredients:
- 1 pound (450g) green beans
- cooking spray
- salt to taste

Directions:

1. Preheat the air fryer to 400 degrees F / 200 degrees C.
2. Add the green beans to a bowl and spray with some low-calorie spray and the best salt ever and combine.
3. Place the beans into the air fryer basket and cook for 6-8 minutes, turning a couple of times during cooking so that they brown evenly.
4. Remove and serve topped with some extra salt and chopped herbs if you like.

Notes

Finer green beans as I use here need 6-8 minutes.

If you are using larger beans then you may need 8-10 minutes.

If you have a small air fryer, then cook beans in 2 batches.

Make sure you top and tail your beans before air frying them.

Make sure the beans are dry before spraying with cooking spray.

If you don't have a cooking spray you can use olive oil but this will increase the calorie count of the portion.

Storage - keep leftovers in an airtight container in the fridge for 4 days.

Air Fryer Chickpeas

Servings: 4
Cooking Time: 15 Minutes

Ingredients:

- 1 (15.5 ounce) can chickpeas, drained and rinsed
- ¾ tablespoon avocado oil
- 2 teaspoons chili-lime seasoning (such as Tajin®)
- ¼ teaspoon garlic powder
- 1 pinch cayenne pepper, or to taste
- salt to taste

Directions:

1. Preheat air fryer to 400 degrees F (200 degrees C). Spray the air fryer basket with cooking spray or use a parchment liner.
2. Place chickpeas on a paper towel-lined plate to dry, patting down with another paper towel on top. Add dried chickpeas to a medium bowl, drizzle with avocado oil, sprinkle with Tajin, garlic powder, and cayenne, and toss to coat.
3. Transfer chickpeas to the air fryer basket, and cook, stirring or shaking halfway through, until you reach your desired crispness, 12 to 15 minutes. Cooking time may vary depending on the brand and size of your air fryer.
4. Season with salt and allow chickpeas to cool slightly.

Cook's Note:

If you don't have avocado oil, use olive oil. Being sure the chickpeas are dry will help them crisp up and the seasoning to stick better. Store the cooled chickpeas in an airtight container at room temperature for up to a week. If they get soft, place them back in the air fryer for a couple minutes to crisp up.

Air Fryer Nachos

Servings: 4
Cooking Time: 10 Minutes

Ingredients:

- 2-3 cups tortilla chips
- 2 cups cheese shredded
- 1 green onion whites and greens separated
- ¼ cup black olives
- ½ cup tomatoes diced
- ¼ cup jalapenos chopped, optional
- 2 tablespoons cilantro chopped, optional

Directions:

1. Place the tortilla chips in a single layer in the air fryer basket making sure to overlap the chips so there are no gaps between them.
2. Top the chips with half of the cheese and whites of the green onion.
3. Add another layer of chips. Top with remaining cheese, green onions, jalapenos, and black olives (if using).
4. Place in the air fryer to 320°F and cook the nachos for 3-5 minutes or until cheese has melted.
5. Remove from the basket and top with diced tomatoes.
6. Serve with salsa and sour cream.

Homemade Air Fryer Tater Tots

Servings: 8
Cooking Time: 20 Minutes

Ingredients:

- 1 16 ounce bag of frozen shredded hash browns
- 2 tablespoons olive oil
- 2 tablespoons flour
- 3 cloves garlic minced
- 1 teaspoon dried Italian seasoning
- ½ teaspoon kosher salt
- ¼ cup grated parmesan cheese

Directions:

1. Pulse hashbrowns in a food processor until finely chopped (don't allow them to become mashed potatoes).
2. Gently mix the potatoes with olive oil, flour, garlic, & seasoning.

3. Scoop tablespoon-sized amounts of the mixture and form into 1" tater tots. Place in the air fryer in a single layer, evenly spaced.
4. Spray them with olive oil or cooking spray. Air fry tater tots at 375°F for 15-18 minutes until crispy and golden brown, shaking the air fryer basket once during cooking.
5. Remove tots from the fryer, and sprinkle with shredded parmesan and seasoning. Serve warm.

Notes

For extra garlicky tater tots add a teaspoon of garlic powder.

For cheesy tots, add ¼-½ cup parmesan cheese to the tater tot mixture.

Store in an airtight container in the fridge for up to 5 days.

Air-fryer Caribbean Wontons

Servings: 2
Cooking Time: 10 Minutes

Ingredients:
- 4 ounces cream cheese, softened
- 1/4 cup sweetened shredded coconut
- 1/4 cup mashed ripe banana
- 2 tablespoons chopped walnuts
- 2 tablespoons canned crushed pineapple
- 1 cup marshmallow creme
- 24 wonton wrappers
- Cooking spray
- SAUCE:
- 1 pound fresh strawberries, hulled
- 1/4 cup sugar
- 1 teaspoon cornstarch
- Confectioners' sugar and ground cinnamon

Directions:
1. Preheat air fryer to 350°. In a small bowl, beat cream cheese until smooth. Stir in coconut, banana, walnuts and pineapple. Fold in marshmallow creme.
2. Position a wonton wrapper with 1 point toward you. Keep remaining wrappers covered with a damp paper towel until ready to use. Place 2 teaspoons filling in the center of wrapper. Moisten edges with water; fold opposite corners together over filling and press to seal. Repeat with remaining wrappers and filling.
3. In batches, arrange wontons in a single layer on greased tray in air-fryer basket; spritz with cooking spray. Cook until golden brown and crisp, 10-12 minutes.
4. Meanwhile, place strawberries in a food processor; cover and process until pureed. In a small saucepan, combine sugar and cornstarch. Stir in pureed strawberries. Bring to a boil; cook and stir until thickened, 2 minutes. If desired, strain mixture, reserving sauce; discard seeds. Sprinkle wontons with confectioners' sugar and cinnamon. Serve with sauce.

BREAKFAST & BRUNCH RECIPES

Air Fryer Falafel

Servings: 16
Cooking Time: 15 Minutes

Ingredients:

- 2 cups dried chickpeas (NOT canned or cooked chickpeas)
- 1 cup red onion, chopped
- 6 garlic cloves, peeled
- 1 cup fresh parsley, leaves and tender stems
- ½ cup fresh cilantro, leaves and tender stems
- ¼ cup fresh dill, stems removed
- 2 teaspoons ground cumin
- 2 teaspoons ground coriander
- 1 teaspoon sea salt, or to taste
- 1 teaspoon black pepper
- ½ teaspoon red pepper flakes (optional)
- 1 ½ tablespoons toasted sesame seeds (optional)
- 1 teaspoon baking powder (optional)
- SERVE WITH: Pita bread, tahini sauce, hummus, tomatoes, cucumber, lettuce, lemon wedges

Directions:

1. The day before you plan to cook the falafel, place the dried chickpeas in a large bowl. Fill the bowl with water, covering the chickpeas by at least 2 inches. Soak for 18-24 hours until softened, then drain the chickpeas well and pat them dry.
2. Add the chickpeas, onion, garlic, herbs, and spices to the bowl of a food processor fitted with a blade. Pulse for 30 seconds, scrape down the sides of the bowl, then process again for 20-30 more seconds until well combined.
3. Transfer the mixture to a bowl, cover it tightly with a lid or plastic wrap, and refrigerate for at least 1 hour or overnight.
4. When ready to cook, remove the bowl from the refrigerator and stir the sesame seeds and baking powder into the mixture.
5. Wet your hands, then scoop heaping tablespoonfuls of the mixture and form it into balls or patties (½ inch in thickness each).
6. Spray the inner basket of the air fryer with cooking spray, then place the falafel in an even layer inside, being sure not to overcrowd. Lightly spray the falafel with cooking spray as well.
7. Air fry at 380 degrees F for 15 minutes, flipping them once halfway through the cook time, until they're golden brown and crispy. Repeat with any remaining falafel balls.

NOTES
If your falafel batter feels loose and won't hold together, add 1 to 1 ½ tablespoons of chickpea flour or all-purpose flour to help bind it.

Breakfast Egg Rolls

Servings: 6
Cooking Time: 15 Minutes

Ingredients:

- 6 large eggs
- 1 tablespoon water
- 1/4 teaspoon kosher salt
- black pepper (to taste)
- 1/2 pound chicken or turkey sausage
- 2 tablespoons chopped green onions
- 2 tablespoons diced red bell pepper
- olive oil spray
- 12 egg roll wrappers
- salsa (optional for dipping)

Directions:

1. Beat eggs with water, salt and black pepper.
2. In a medium nonstick skillet, cook sausage over medium heat until no longer pink, 4 minutes, breaking into crumbles; drain.
3. Stir in scallions and peppers and cook 2 minutes. Set aside on a dish.
4. Heat the skillet over medium heat and spray with oil.

5. Pour in egg mixture and cook stirring until eggs are fluffy and cooked. Stir in sausage mixture.
6. Place 1 eggroll wrapper on a clean, dry work surface with corners positioned like a diamond.
7. Add 1/4 cup of the egg mixture on the bottom third of the wrapper.
8. Carefully lift the bottom point nearest to you and wrap it around the filling. Dip your finger into a small bowl of water and run it along the edges of the wrapper.
9. Fold the left and right corners in toward the center and continue to roll into a tight cylinder.
10. Repeat with remaining filling and wrappers.
11. Spray all sides of the egg rolls with oil and rub with your hands to evenly coat.
12. Preheat air fryer to 370F.
13. Cook egg rolls in batches for 10 minutes, turning halfway or until golden brown and crisp.
14. Serve immediately with salsa, if desired.
15. Egg Roll Oven Recipe:
16. Bake 400F in a preheated oven 12 to 16 minutes, flipping halfway.
17. From frozen, 375F 18 to 20 minutes, flipping halfway.

Air-fryer Hash Brown

Servings: 4
Cooking Time: 20 Minutes

Ingredients:
- 500g brushed potatoes, peeled, grated
- 1 tsp onion powder
- 2 tbs extra virgin olive oil
- 5ml olive oil cooking spray
- 1/3 cup Greek-style yoghurt (to serve)
- 1/4 cup small continental parsley leaves (to serve)

Directions:
1. Preheat air fryer to 170°C for 2 minutes.
2. Place potato in a large clean tea towel and squeeze out as much moisture as possible. Place potato in a large bowl with onion powder and extra virgin olive oil, then stir to combine. Season with pepper.
3. Lightly spray air-fryer basket with oil. Spoon potato mixture into basket and press with a spatula to form a 1.5cm-thick round. Slide pan and basket into air fryer. Set timer for 20 minutes, turning hash brown halfway through cooking, or until golden. Stand for 10 minutes, then transfer to a board. Serve topped with yoghurt
4. and parsley

Tinga Cauliflower Tacos

Servings: 3

Ingredients:
- 2 small or 1 large cauliflower, greens removed and set aside, cut into small florets
- 2 tbsp olive oil
- 1 tsp dried orgeano
- 1 tsp chipotle powder
- Salt and pepper
- For the sauce
- 450g vine tomatoes, stems removed and washed
- 3 cloves garlic, with skin smashed to loosen skin
- 1/2 red or white onion, whole
- 2 tbsp chipotle paste
- 1 tsp brown sugar
- 1 tbsp fresh lime juice
- Salt and pepper
- For the slaw
- Greens from cauliflower, washed and shredded
- 5 radish, sliced thinly
- 150g red cabbage, shredded
- 1 spring onion
- 1 red or green chilli
- 2 tbsp vegan mayo
- 1-2 tbsp fresh lime juice
- 5g fresh coriander, chopped
- 1/2 tsp brown sugar
- To taste salt and pepper
- To serve
- Pack fresh corn tortillas

- Guacamole
- Salsa
- Vegan sour cream
- Chillies
- COOKING MODE
- When entering cooking mode - We will enable your screen to stay 'always on' to avoid any unnecessary interruptions whilst you cook!

Directions:
1. Toss all the ingredients together for the cauliflower, you will need to cook this in two batches
2. Place ½ ingredients for cauliflower in drawer 1. Turn on the Ninja Foodi Dual Zone Air Fryer, select "1", select "AIR FRY", set the temperature to 180 and the time to 10-12 minutes
3. Place the tomatoes, garlic and onion in to drawer 2. Select "2", press "ROAST ", set the time to 15 minutes and the temp to 200C. Press "SYNC" and then "Start"
4. When sauce is done remove and place in a food processor with chipotle paste, brown sugar, lime juice and set it to chop
5. Add the rest of cauliflower in to drawer 1 of the Ninja Foodi Dual Zone Air Fryer. Select "1", select "AIR FRY", set the temperature to 180 and the time to 10-12 minutes
6. Add the tortillas to drawer 2 , select "2", select "BAKE", set the temperature to 180 and the time to 2-3 minutes. Press "SYNC" and select "Start"
7. Once the cauliflower is all cooked, toss with ¾ of sauce and ROAST at 180 for 5 minutes to warm through, toss as it cooks. Toss remaining through once heated to be sure it is nice and saucy
8. Toss all ingredients together for slaw
9. Serve on tortillas with slaw and guacamole and salsa, vegan sour cream

Naan Breads
Ingredients:
- 1 cup flour
- 1 tsp baking powder
- 1/2 tsp salt
- 1/2 cup full cream yoghurt

Directions:
1. Mix up dry ingredients and add in enough yoghurt to make a dough. Knead for a few minutes (dough will still be slightly sticky) cut in balls and rest dough for 10 minutes at least.
2. Roll out very thin and place in drawer and set to 185C for 4-6 minutes till puffy and fully cooked.
3. While hot, brush with garlic butter and Enjoy!

Air Fryer Spaghetti Squash
Servings: 4
Cooking Time: 30 Minutes
Ingredients:
- 1 spaghetti squash 3 lbs
- 1 tablespoon olive oil
- ¼ teaspoon salt
- ¼ teaspoon pepper

Directions:
1. Preheat air fryer to 370°F.
2. Cut spaghetti squash in half lengthwise, scoop out the seeds with a spoon.
3. Coat the cut side of the squash with olive oil and season with salt and pepper.
4. Place them in the air fryer cut side up and cook for 25-30 minutes or until fork tender.
5. Remove from the air fryer and scrape the flesh with a fork creating long strands.

Air Fryer Hand Pies

Ingredients:

- 2 Fuji apples, peeled, cored, and cut into 1/4-inch dice (2 cups)
- 3/4 cup raspberries
- 2 tbsp light brown sugar, lightly packed
- 1 tbsp granulated sugar, plus additional for sprinkling
- 1/4 tsp ground cinnamon
- pinch kosher salt
- 1 tbsp apple juice or cider
- 1-1/2 tsp cornstarch mixed with 1 tsp water (slurry)
- 1 package (2 rounds) refrigerated pie crusts
- 1 large egg yolk mixed with 1 tsp water (egg wash)

Directions:

1. In a medium pot, stir together apples, raspberries, sugars, cinnamon, salt, and apple juice or cider. Bring to a simmer over medium heat, cover, and reduce heat to low. Cook, stirring occasionally, until apples begin to soften but still retain their shape, about 15 mins.
2. Add the slurry to the filling mixture. Increase heat to medium and cook for 1-2 mins, until thickened. Remove from heat and cool to room temperature.
3. While the filling is cooling, unroll pie crusts. Cut the dough into 4-inch circles using a cookie cutter, re-rolling the scraps as needed. You'll need 12 circles.
4. Place 1 tbsp of filling on the center of each circle. Brush the edges of the dough with water, fold the dough in half over the filling, and press to seal. Don't overfill.
5. Use a fork to crimp the sealed edges. Lightly brush the pies with egg wash and use the tip of a paring knife to pierce two small slits in the top of each pie. Sprinkle the tops with sugar.
6. Preheat KRUPS air fryer to 320°F. Add the pies in a single layer, 6 at a time, and bake for 15 minutes, until the tops are golden. (Refrigerate the pies that aren't being baked so the dough doesn't become too soft.) Remove to a wire rack to cool.
7. Repeat with the remaining pies and enjoy!

Air Fryer Tex Mex Egg Rolls

Servings: 20
Cooking Time: 11 Minutes

Ingredients:

- 1 pound lean ground beef
- 1 onion finely diced
- 1 green pepper diced
- 1 package taco seasoning plus water as per package
- 2 tablespoons salsa
- 20 egg roll wrappers mine were 5"x5"
- 2 cups cheese shredded and divided (cheddar, Monterey jack, tex mex blend all work well). Cheese sticks also work great.
- oil for frying optional

Directions:

1. Brown ground beef and onions until no pink remains.
2. Stir in green peppers, taco seasoning, salsa, and water (as required on the seasoning package). Cook until the water evaporates.
3. Lay out each egg roll wrapper (in a diamond facing you). Place 1 ½ tablespoons each of cheese and taco filling in the center of each wrapper.
4. Fold diagonally, fold sides in and roll up sealing the tip with a little bit of the water. Brush the outside of each egg roll with a little bit of vegetable oil or spray with cooking spray.
5. Place in the air fryer basket 3-4 at a time and cook at 390°F for 8 minutes. Flip and cook for an additional 3 minutes.

Notes
To Deep Fry Egg Rolls in Oil:
Preheat oil to 350°F.
Carefully fry each egg roll for about 4-5 minutes or until browned and crispy.
Remove and place on a paper towel-lined paper to cool slightly before serving.

CAUTION: It is very important to make sure the wrappers are fully sealed when deep frying. Any ingredients that leak out have the chance to cause splattering which can cause severe burns.
To Make in the Oven:
Assemble taco egg rolls, spray with cooking spray.
Place in a single layer on a parchment-lined baking sheet.
Bake at 350°F until brown and crispy, flipping halfway through baking.

Five Cheese Pull Apart Bread

Ingredients:
- 1 bread loaf, medium
- 7 tbsp butter
- 2 tsp garlic puree
- ½ cup cheddar cheese
- 4 oz. goat cheese
- ½ cup mozzarella cheese
- ½ cup Gouda cheese
- 4 oz. brie cheese
- 2 tsp chives
- salt and pepper, to taste

Directions:
1. Grate your hard cheese into 3 different piles and set aside.
2. In a saucepan, melt the butter on medium heat. Add in the chives, salt, pepper and garlic. Cook for another 2 minutes, mix well and then set aside.
3. Using a bread knife, create little slits into your bread. In each of the little slits cover with the garlic butter mixture until they are all covered. Then, insert the goat and brie cheese in all of the slits to give them a lovely creamy taste.
4. Spread the cheddar, mozzarella and Gouda cheese over the tops and fill the cracks with them. Place your standard rack in the air fryer and place the bread on top. Air fry it at 350° for 4 minutes, or until the cheese is melted and the bread is warm.

Air Fryer Breakfast Burritos

Servings: 6
Cooking Time: 5 Minutes

Ingredients:
- 6 medium flour tortillas
- 6 scrambled eggs
- ½ lb ground sausage – browned
- ½ bell pepper – minced
- ⅓ cup bacon bits
- ½ cup shredded cheese
- oil for spraying

Directions:
1. Combine the scrambled eggs, cooked sausage, bell pepper, bacon bits, and cheese in a large bowl. Stir to combine.
2. Spoon about a ½ cup of the mixture into the center of a flour tortilla.
3. Fold in the sides & then roll.
4. Repeat with the remaining ingredients.
5. Place the filled burritos into the air fryer basket & spray liberally with oil.
6. Cook at 330 degrees for 5 minutes or until hot and the tortilla is slightly cripsy.

Air Fryer 2-ingredient Sweet Potato Rolls No Yeast

Servings: 6
Cooking Time: 14 Minutes

Ingredients:
- 1 cup (240 ml) cooked sweet potato , mashed
- 1 cup (240 ml) self rising flour
- oil spray , for basket & rolls
- EQUIPMENT
- Air Fryer

Directions:
1. In bowl, combine sweet potato and flour. Stir with a fork until a dough ball forms. Make sure to scrape all the flour and sweet potato along the sides of the bowl.
2. On a lightly floured surface, knead the soft dough ball for about 1 minute, or until smooth. Don't keep adding too much flour to the dough or else it will be tough and

hard. You want to keep the dough soft and pliable, so don't over-knead it.

3. Cut the dough into 6 equal pieces. Roll the dough between your hands to form 6 balls. Let the dough balls rest for about 30 minutes (they will also rise slightly).

4. Spray air fryer basket or tray with oil. Gently place dough balls in the basket, evenly spaced apart. Lightly spray the tops of the dough balls with oil.

5. Air Fry at 330°F/165°C for 10-14 minutes or until the rolls are cooked through. Allow to cool and serve with butter or as small slider or sandwich buns.

Taco Crunchwrap

Servings: 1
Cooking Time: 5 Minutes

Ingredients:

- 1 large burrito (10 inch) size tortilla
- 2 tbsp fat free refried beans
- 1/4 cup extra lean ground beef seasoned with taco seasoning
- 2 tbsp reduced fat shredded cheese
- 2 tbsp nacho cheese dip i use the fritos brand cheddar or jalapeno cheese dip, but you can find multiple different brands in the chip aisle! Rico's nacho cheese is also delicious.
- 1 tbsp non fat greek yogurt I prefer Fage. You also can use sour cream.
- 8 bite size tortilla chips I use the Tostitos brand, but any kind of chip will do
- 2 tbsp finely chopped onions and lettuce
- 1 tbsp favorite salsa or a couple finely chopped cherry tomatos work too!
- cooking spray (i prefer to use Avocado oil cooking spray)

Directions:

1. Make a cut into the middle of the tortilla and only go to the middle. (Pictures in blog post will describe this best, once you see it, you won't forget it!)

2. Look at the tortilla and divide the ingredients into four quadrants. On the left half spread the cheese dip then pile on the broken tortilla chips in one quadrant and ground beef in the other quadrant. On the remaining spread nonfat greek yogurt in one of the quadrants then add lettuce, onion, salsa (or tomatoes). In the last quadrant spread the refriend beans then add the shredded cheese on top.

3. Fold: First fold the bottom left quadrant up over the upper left quadrant then fold that over onto the upper right quadrant then fold all of those back down onto the bottom right quadrant. The end of result will look like a triangle.

4. I know this might not make sense in written form so if you haven't seen the tortilla folding method yet please check out the step by step photos on my blog post above. It will make much better sense. Once you do it once you won't forget it!

5. You don't have to heat this up, but I would especially if your filling ingredients aren't warmed up. I do prefer it warmed up.

6. Air Fryer: Spray each side lightly with a little bit of cooking spray then place in the air fryer and heat until lightly golden brown at 350 degrees for about 5-6 minutes.

7. Skillet: Heat skillet over medium heat and spray each side of the wrap lightly with cooking spray. Heat each side for 2-3 minutes or until lightly golden brown.

Toaster Strudel In The Air Fryer

Servings: 4
Cooking Time: 6 Minutes

Ingredients:

- 1 Package of Toaster Strudel with icing

Directions:

1. Place your frozen toaster strudel into your air fryer.

2. Cook it at 350 degrees for 6 minutes. The size and brand of your air fryer will vary this time slightly.

3. Remove from your air fryer, drizzle icing over it, and serve.

NOTES: There is no need to preheat your air fryer or grease it.

Air Fryer Scrambled Eggs

Servings: 2

Cooking Time: 7 Minutes

Ingredients:

- 1 tablespoon butter
- 4 large eggs
- salt and freshly ground black pepper to taste

Directions:

1. Preheat the air fryer to 300 degrees F (150 degrees C). Place silicone liner into the air fryer basket and set butter on top.
2. Allow butter to melt, 1 to 2 minutes. Increase heat to 310 degrees F (154 degrees C).
3. Meanwhile, combine eggs and salt in a bowl and whisk until well combined. Pour egg mixture into silicone liner.
4. Cook eggs for 2 minutes. Stir the eggs with a spatula and continue cooking until eggs are set to your liking, 4 to 5 minutes. Sprinkle with pepper before serving.

Air Fryer Cherry Cream Cheese Croissants

Servings: 8

Cooking Time: 5 Minutes

Ingredients:

- flour for dusting
- 1 (8 ounce) package refrigerated crescent roll dough (such as Pillsbury®)
- 1 (8 ounce) tub cream cheese
- 1 (15 ounce) can pitted sour cherries, drained
- cooking spray
- ground cinnamon to taste

Directions:

1. Lightly dust a work surface with flour. Unroll crescent dough and divide into triangles along the perforated lines.
2. Spread each triangle with cream cheese.
3. Drop 3 or 4 cherries on the wider portion of each crescent dough triangle. Carefully roll up each crescent, making sure the cherries stay tucked in. Fold down the ends of each roll slightly so it forms a crescent shape.
4. Spray the basket of the air fryer with non stick cooking spray spray. Carefully set the croissants into the basket.
5. Set air fryer to 400 degrees F (200 degrees C).
6. Air fry croissants until puffed up and lightly browned, about 5 minutes. Check to make sure croissants are not sticking to each other and that they are not overly browned. Continue cooking for 2 to 3 minutes longer, making sure they do not get too done.
7. Transfer croissants to a plate and sprinkle with cinnamon.

Cook's Note:

You can use cherry pie filling instead of canned cherries.

Scallion Pancake

Servings: 8

Ingredients:

- 1/4 c. low-sodium soy sauce
- 2 tbsp. rice vinegar
- 2 tsp. sambal-style chili paste
- 1 tsp. sugar
- 1 2-inch piece fresh ginger, peeled and cut into matchsticks
- 1 14-oz pkg. round dumpling wrappers
- 1/4 c. toasted sesame oil
- 8 scallions, chopped (11/2 cups)
- 8 tbsp. canola oil

Directions:

1. In small bowl, whisk together soy sauce, rice vinegar, chili paste, and sugar; stir in ginger and set aside.
2. On cutting board, place 1 dumpling wrapper. Light brush top with sesame oil and scatter 2 teaspoons scallions on top. Top with second dumpling wrapper, pressing to adhere. Repeat with sesame oil, scallions, and wrappers until you have a stack of 6 wrappers. Repeat with remaining ingredients to make a total of 8 stacks of 6 wrappers each.

3. Working with 1 at a time, using a rolling pin, roll out each stack of wrappers to 6-inch-diameter circle, turning and flipping over as necessary. Repeat until all stacks are rolled out.
4. Heat 1 Tbsp canola oil in medium skillet on medium. Cook 1 pancake at a time until golden brown, 1 to 2 minutes per side. Repeat with remaining oil and pancake stacks. Serve sprinkled with any remaining scallions and with ginger-chili sauce for dipping.
5. AIR FRYER SHORTCUT SCALLION PANCAKES: Follow steps 1-2 (do not roll out stacks of wrappers). Heat air fryer to 400°F. Brush both sides of stacks liberally with canola oil. Place 4 stacks in air-fryer basket, spacing apart so they don't touch. Air-fry 3 to 4 minutes. Using tongs, flip and air-fry until golden brown and crispy, 3 to 4 minutes more. Repeat with remaining stacks. Sprinkle pancakes with more scallions and serve with ginger-chili sauce for dipping.

Air Fryer Reuben Stromboli

Servings: 6
Cooking Time: 15 Minutes

Ingredients:
- 12 ounces fresh pizza dough
- 1 tablespoon Thousand Island dressing
- 1/2 pound thinly sliced corned beef
- 6 slices swiss cheese
- 1 cup sauerkraut, squeezed in paper towels to get rid of liquid
- Thousand Island for serving
- cooking spray
- 1/4 teaspoon garlic salt

Directions:
1. Roll dough into a rectangles about 10 inches long. Spread Thousand Island over the top.
2. Layer the corned beef, sauerkraut, and cheese, leaving a 1-inch border.
3. Starting on one long side, roll the dough up. Stretch the ends and tuck them under. Position so seam is on bottom. Lightly spray top with cooking spray and sprinkle with garlic salt.
4. Set Air Fryer to 350 for 15 minutes. Let preheat for 2 minutes. Place stromboli in the Air Fryer basket and Air Fry for the remaning 13 minutes.
5. Cut into slices and serve with Thousand Island dressing.
6. Notes
7. Use the cooking time as an estimate. Some air fryers cook faster or slower than others. At the end of 15 minutes, make a small cup into the stromboli. If it is still doughy inside, cook it longer.

Air Fryer Pierogies With Onions

Servings: 2
Cooking Time: 22 Minutes

Ingredients:
- 14 frozen pierogies
- 1 small onion
- 1 tablespoon oil
- small pinch of sugar
- spraying oil

Directions:
1. Heat a large pot halfway full with water on high heat to a boil. Once boiling, cook pierogies for 5 minutes and remove from water/drain.
2. While water is heating up, slice the onion into long slices.
3. Place oil in an air fryer pan and cook on 300 for 1 minute.
4. Add onion to the pan, mix to coat, and cook on 300 degrees for 12-15 minutes, stirring every 3 minutes. Add a small pinch of sugar to them after cooking for 6 minutes and mix to coat.
5. Remove from the air fryer and set aside.
6. Place pierogies in an air fryer and cook at 350 degrees for 4 minutes.
7. Spritz the tops with oil and increase the temperature to 400. Cook for another 4-5 minutes until tops are golden brown.
8. Combine pierogies and onions and enjoy immediately.

Reuben Egg Rolls

Servings: 6
Cooking Time: 10 Minutes

Ingredients:
- 6 egg roll wrappers
- 6 slices corned beef
- 6 slices swiss cheese cut into 1" strips
- 1 ¼ cups sauerkraut drained and squeezed dry
- 1 teaspoon caraway seeds optional
- 1 cup Thousand Island Dressing divided use
- oil for frying or air frying

Directions:
1. Preheat oil to 375°F or air fryer to 380°F.
2. Stack corned beef and cut into thin strips.
3. Lay egg roll wrappers with a corner pointed toward you. Divide corned beef, swiss cheese, and sauerkraut over the wrappers. Drizzle each with 1 tablespoon of the dressing and sprinkle with caraway seeds if using.
4. Dip your finger in water and run it along the edges of the egg roll wrapper.
5. Fold the two sides in and tightly roll the egg roll. Seal the edges.
6. If air frying, brush each egg roll with vegetable oil (or spray with cooking spray) and place in a single layer, seam side down. See below for oven or deep fryer instructions.
7. Cook 7 minutes. Flip and cook an additional 3-5 minutes or until crispy. Serve with remaining dressing for dipping.

Notes
To Bake in the Oven: Place egg rolls on a baking sheet sprayed with pan release at 350° F for 8 minutes. Flip them over and bake until they are browned, another 5-7 minutes.
To Deep Fry preheat oil to 350°F. Gently place egg rolls in preheated oil turning as needed until browned and crispy, about 4-5 minutes.
Egg Rolls can be prepared up to 2 days in advance and refrigerated or frozen. If cooking from frozen, add 2-3 minutes cooking time depending on the method used.

Peanut Butter Breakfast Oatmeal Bowl

Servings: 1
Cooking Time: 5 Minutes

Ingredients:
- 1 medium banana (sliced)
- 1/3 cup quick or rolled oats
- 1/4 cup raspberries
- 1/4 cup blueberries
- 1 tablespoon chopped almonds
- 1 teaspoon chia seeds
- 1 tablespoon creamy peanut butter (melted 30 to 60 seconds in the microwave.)

Directions:
1. Mash half of the banana with a fork.
2. Combine 2/3 cup water, oats and the mashed banana in a small saucepan.
3. Cook over medium-low heat, stirring occasionally, until the oats have thickened and softened, about 1 to 5 minutes, depending on the oats you use.
4. Transfer to a bowl and top with the remaining banana sliced, raspberries, blueberries, almonds and chia seeds then drizzle with the melted peanut butter.

Notes
Double or triple for more servings.

Air Fryer French Toast Sticks

Servings: 4
Cooking Time: 8 Minutes

Ingredients:
- 4-6 pieces bread (allow it to sit out for 2-3 hours before using)
- 2 eggs
- 3 tbsp granulated white sugar
- 2 tsp cinnamon

Directions:
1. Mix the cinnamon and sugar together in a small bowl or plate and set aside.
2. Stack the bread and then use a serated knife to cut the slices into thirds.
3. Whisk the eggs together and pour them into a rimmed plate.

4. Dip the bread pieces into the egg and then dip into the cinnamon and sugar.
5. Place the bread into the prepared Air Fryer basket in a single layer with an inch or two between slices.
6. Air Fryer the bread pieces for 8-9 minutes on 370 degrees Fahrenheit, flipping them halfway through.
7. Remove from the Air Fryer and serve immediately.

Air Fryer Croutons

Servings: 3
Cooking Time: 8 Minutes

Ingredients:
- ½ loaf stale bread (4 cups cubed bread) (sourdough works great!)
- 3 tablespoons melted butter
- 1 teaspoon italian seasoning
- ½ teaspoon garlic powder
- ½ teaspoon salt

Directions:
1. Preheat your air fryer to 350 F.
2. Cut bread into ½" -¾" cubes and place into a large bowl.
3. Drizzle bread with melted butter, then sprinkle italian seasoning, garlic powder, and salt on top.
4. Toss until all bread cubes are well coated.
5. Place into your air fryer and cook for 6-8 minutes, or until croutons are golden brown on the outside.

Air Fryer French Onion Tarts

Servings: 2
Cooking Time: 30 Minutes

Ingredients:
- 2 sheets shortcrust pastry, just thawed
- 1 tbsp olive oil
- 1 small brown onion, thinly sliced
- 75g cream cheese
- 2 tbsp sour cream
- 25g (¼ cup) grated cheddar
- 3 large eggs
- Chopped fresh chives, to serve (optional)
- Select all ingredients

Directions:
1. Lightly grease two 15cm fluted tartlet tins.
2. Place 1 sheet of pastry on a lightly floured bench. Top with the remaining pastry sheet. Sprinkle with a little flour and roll out to 3mm thickness. Cut in half diagonally. Ease 1 half into 1 prepared tart tin. Repeat with remaining pastry half and tart tin. Trim excess pastry. Line the pastry cases with baking paper and fill with pastry weights or rice. Place in the basket of an XXL airfryer and air fry at 200C for 6 minutes. Remove the paper and baking beans or rice and and air fry for a further 2 minutes.
3. Meanwhile, heat the oil in a frying pan over medium heat. Add onion and cook, stirring occasionally, for 10 minutes or until golden and caramelised. Set aside to cool slightly.
4. Combine cream cheese, sour cream, cheddar and 1 egg in a bowl. Add the onion. Stir to combine. Season. Divide the mixture between tart cases. Make a small well in the centre of 1 tart. Crack an egg into the well. Repeat with remaining tart and egg. Season with pepper.
5. Air fry at 170C for 10-12 minutes or until just cooked. Leave in the air fryer to cool for 5 minutes or until the egg is cooked to your liking.
6. Sprinkle with chives, if using, to serve.

Air Fryer Egg Bites

Servings: 6
Cooking Time: 10 Minutes

Ingredients:

- 6 large eggs
- 1 tbsp milk
- 4 slices bacon crumbled
- 1/2 cup cheddar cheese shredded
- 1/2 tsp salt
- 1/4 tsp pepper
- 1 green onion chopped

Directions:

1. In a large bowl, combine the eggs and milk, and whisk together.
2. Add in the crumbled bacon, grated cheddar cheese, onions, and seasonings, stirring to combine.
3. Equally divide the egg mixture into silicone cups, about ⅔ full, leaving room for them to rise.
4. Place in the air fryer basket, or on a baking sheet if you have tray air fryer.
5. Cook at 300 degrees F for 8-10 minutes.

Air Fryer Banana Bread

Servings: 4-6
Cooking Time: 35 Minutes

Ingredients:

- 3 very ripe, medium bananas (±285g)
- 100g / ⅓ cup maple syrup
- 65g / ⅓ cup coconut oil, melted
- 2 extra-large eggs
- 60ml / ¼ cup milk
- 1 tsp vanilla extract
- 225g / 1 ½ cups flour
- 1 tsp baking powder
- 1 tsp ground cinnamon
- Pinch sea salt
- 50g dark chocolate, roughly chopped
- 50g pecan nuts, roughly chopped

Directions:

1. Grease a 20 x 20cm baking tin.
2. Mash bananas in a large bowl.
3. Add the maple syrup, coconut oil, eggs, milk and vanilla extract. Whisk well.
4. In a separate bowl combine the flour, baking powder, ground cinnamon and salt. Whisk.
5. Add the dark chocolate and pecans and mix well.
6. Pour the wet ingredients into the dry ingredients and mix together.
7. Pour the mixture into the prepared tin.
8. Select Bake for 30 minutes at 160°C.
9. Remove the banana bread from the tin, return it to the Vortex's inner basket and select Bake again at 160°C for another 5 minutes.
10. Allow the banana bread to cool before slicing and serving.

DESSERTS RECIPES

Air Fryer Cheesecake

Servings: 6
Cooking Time: 1 Hour

Ingredients:

- Crust
- ¾ cup graham cracker crumbs
- 2 tablespoons granulated sugar
- 2 tablespoons butter melted
- A dash of salt
- Cheesecake Filling
- 16 ounces cream cheese softened
- ½ cup sour cream
- ¾ cup granulated sugar
- 2 large eggs room temperature
- 1 teaspoon lemon zest
- 1 teaspoon vanilla extract

Directions:

1. Crust
2. Grease a 6-7 inch springform pan with cooking spray. Place a parchment round in the bottom.
3. Combine the graham cracker crumbs with the melted butter and salt until it resembles wet sand. Press into the bottom of the pan, use your fingers or a flat-bottomed glass or measuring cup to press it in. If you're using a 6-inch pan you may omit a tablespoon or two of the crust if desired.
4. Bake in the airfryer at 275 degrees fahrenheit for 10 minutes. Let cool completely.
5. Cheesecake Filling
6. Use a stand mixer or hand mixer to beat the softened cream cheese and sour cream until smooth. Add the sugar and beat again until combined, scraping down the sides and bottom of the bowl as needed.
7. Add the eggs one at a time, mixing each one just until incorporated. Add the lemon zest and vanilla and beat until combined and smooth.
8. Pour the batter over the cooled crust and bake at 285 degrees fahrenheit for 30 minutes. After 30 minutes, bake at 250 degrees fahrenheit for 15-20 minutes more, until the cheesecake is set but still has a little wobble to it.
9. Crack open the airfryer and leave the cheesecake inside for 30-60 minutes, until the airfryer has cooled.
10. Chill the cheesecake in the fridge for 4 hours or overnight before removing from the pan and serving.

Air Fryer Gaytime Custard Doughnuts

Servings: 16
Cooking Time: 15 Minutes

Ingredients:

- 180g block Cadbury Caramilk chocolate, chopped
- 125ml (½ cup) warm milk
- 150g (1 cup) pure icing sugar
- 175g pkt Arnott's TV Snacks Original, crushed
- Golden Gaytime filling
- 600g bought vanilla custard
- 50g (⅓ cup) cornflour
- 4 x Golden Gaytime ice-creams, sticks removed
- 3 tbsp malt powder
- Doughnuts
- 300ml milk, warmed
- 7g sachet dried yeast
- 70g (1/3 cup) caster sugar
- 4 cups (600g) plain flour, plus 40g (¼ cup) extra, to dust
- 1 egg
- 1 egg yolk
- 125g unsalted butter, chopped, at room temperature
- Select all Ingredients:

Directions:

1. To make the doughnuts, pour the milk into a bowl. Add the yeast and 1 tablespoon

caster sugar and whisk to combine. Place mixture in a warm spot for 5-10 minutes or until foaming.

2. Place flour and remaining sugar into the bowl of a stand mixer fitted with the dough hook attachment. Pour in the yeast mixture. Add the egg, egg yolk and butter. Beat for 8-10 minutes or until dough comes together in a ball and is smooth and elastic (if the dough is loose or a bit too sticky, add the extra 40g (¼ cup) of flour, 1 tablespoon at a time, until dough comes together in a ball). Turn dough onto a lightly floured surface. Knead for 1-2 minutes to bring it together. Transfer to a lightly greased bowl, cover with a clean tea towel and leave in a warm spot to rise for 1 hour or until mixture has doubled in size.

3. Meanwhile, prepare the filling. Pour 125ml (½ cup) custard into a saucepan. Add the cornflour and stir until smooth. Add the remaining custard and ice-cream. Place saucepan over medium-high heat and cook, stirring for 10 mins until thickened. Remove from heat. Add the malt powder and whisk to combine. Cover surface with plastic wrap and set aside for 10 minutes to cool slightly. Spoon into a piping bag fitted with a 0.5mm round nozzle. Place in the fridge until required.

4. Turn the doughnut dough onto a lightly floured surface. Knead for a 1-2 minutes. Divide into 16 pieces (weighing approximately 80g each). Gently knead each piece and shape into a ball. Arrange on a lightly floured baking tray, allowing a little room between each ball to expand. Cover with a clean tea towel and set aside, in a warm place, for 30 minutes to rise.

5. Place a cooling rack over a baking tray. Place 4 doughnuts into the basket of an air fryer. Spray doughnuts with oil. Cook at 180°C for 8 minutes or until golden and cooked through. Transfer to prepared rack. Repeat with remaining doughnuts. Make a small incision into the base of each doughnut. Insert nozzle of piping bag into the incision and gently squeeze to fill each doughnut with 2 tablespoonfuls filling.

6. Place chocolate and half the milk in a heatproof bowl over a saucepan of simmering water (make sure the bowl doesn't touch the water). Stir until chocolate has melted and mixture is smooth. Add icing sugar and stir to combine. Gradually add remaining milk. Pour glaze over doughnuts. Sprinkle doughnuts with the crushed biscuits to serve.

Air Fryer Molten Lava Cakes

Ingredients:
- 110g butter
- 200g chocolate
- 2 large eggs
- 2 egg yolks
- 75g sugar
- 1 tsp vanilla essence
- 1/4 cup flour

Directions:
1. Grease 6 ramekins and dust with cocoa powder. Leave aside.

2. In a bowl melt the butter and chocolate in a bowl until the chocolate is melted (20 second intervals). Mix together until combined. When the mixture has cooled down slightly add in the eggs, mix, and then add in the egg yokes. Mix until combined and add in the flour, sugar and vanilla. Once the batter is smooth pour into the ramekins about half way.

3. Heat the air fryer to 200 degrees Celsius for 8 minutes. Once heated add in the ramekins. After 8 minutes check the cakes and if you like them runny remove with a thick cloth. You can bake further to 9-10 minutes as well. Once you remove from the air fryer the cakes need to be removed from the ramekins as soon as possible or they will continue to cook. Loosen the sides with a knife and gently tilt them out.

4. Serve immediately with ice cream, fresh cream or just as is. Enjoy

Apple Pie In The Air Fryer

Ingredients:
- 4 tablespoons butter
- 6 tablespoons brown sugar
- 1 teaspoon ground cinnamon
- 2 medium Granny Smith apples, diced
- 1 teaspoon cornstarch
- 2 teaspoons cold water
- ½ (14 ounce) package pastry for a 9-inch double crust pie
- cooking spray
- ½ tablespoon grape-seed oil
- ¼ cup powdered sugar
- 1 teaspoon milk, or more as needed

Directions:
1. Combine apples, butter, brown sugar, and cinnamon in a non-stick skillet. Cook over medium heat until apples have softened, about 5 minutes.
2. Dissolve cornstarch in cold water. Stir into apple mixture and cook until sauce thickens, about 1 minute. Remove apple pie filling from heat and set aside to cool while you prepare the crust.
3. Unroll pie crust on a lightly floured surface and roll out slightly to smooth the surface of the dough. Cut the dough into rectangles small enough so that 2 can fit in your air fryer at one time. Repeat with remaining crust until you have 8 equal rectangles, re-rolling some of the scraps of dough if needed.
4. Wet the outer edges of 4 rectangles with water and place some apple filling in the center about 1/2-inch from the edges. Roll out the remaining 4 rectangles so that they are slightly larger than the filled ones. Place these rectangles on top of the filling; crimp the edges with a fork to seal. Cut 4 small slits in the tops of the pies.
5. Brush the tops of 2 pies with grapeseed oil and transfer pies to into your air fryer.

6. Close your air fryer oven door and set the temperature to 385 degrees F (195 degrees C). Bake until golden brown, about 8 minutes. Remove pies from the basket and repeat with the remaining 2 pies.
7. Mix together powdered sugar and milk in a small bowl. Brush glaze on warm pies and allow to dry. Serve pies warm or at room temperature.
8. Enjoy!

Air Fryer Ice Cream Cookie Sandwich

Ingredients:
- 1 1/3 c Flour
- 1/3 c Coconut Sugar
- 1/4 c Brown Sugar
- 1 1/2 sticks of Butter
- 4 tbsp Honey
- 3 tbsp Whole Milk
- 1 tbsp Cocoa Powder
- 1 tsp Vanilla Essence
- 1c Chocolate Chips

Directions:
1. Add Butter and Sugars into a large mixing bowl - using an electric beater, mix the Sugar and Butter together thoroughly.
2. Next, Add Flour, Honey, Cocoa Powder, Vanilla, and Milk - Mix well!
3. To get the best results, use your hands! coat in flour and combine.
4. Add the Chocolate Chips a bit at a time.
5. Make about 12- 17 balls of cookie dough
6. Place some Parchment paper into your Air Fryer to prevent the cookies from sticking.
7. Arrange cookies about 2 inches apart.
8. Cook for 15 minutes at 350°
9. Bonus Round!
10. In your Blender add 1 cup of Heavy Whipping Cream, 1 cup of Half and Half, 1/4 cup Sugar, 1 whole Vanilla Bean, 1/2 tsp of Salt, and 4 cups of Ice.
11. Blend until mixture becomes, Ice Cream!
12. Enjoy!

Air Fryer Muffins

Servings: 6-8

Cooking Time: 15 Minutes

Ingredients:

- 60ml vegetable oil
- 75g natural yogurt
- 1 egg
- 2 tbsp milk
- 100g golden caster sugar
- 150g self-raising flour
- ¼ tsp bicarbonate of soda
- 75g blueberries, chocolate chips or dried fruit

Directions:

1. Heat the air fryer on 160C for 2 mins. Mix the oil, yogurt, egg and milk in a large bowl, then fold in the sugar, flour and bicarbonate of soda and combine well. Fold in the blueberries, chocolate chips or dried fruit, if using. Spoon the mixture into silicone cases or an air fryer muffin tin filled with paper cases to three-quarters full. You should be able to make 6-8 muffins, but you may have to bake them in batches.
2. Place the cases or tin in the air fryer basket and cook for 12-15 mins until the muffins are golden brown and a skewer inserted into the centre comes out clean.

Corned Beef Mini Pot Pies

Servings: 4

Cooking Time: 9 Minutes

Ingredients:

- 3 tablespoons unsalted butter
- ¼ cup fennel bulb, finely chopped
- 2 garlic cloves, minced
- 2 small gold potatoes, small diced
- ½ carrot, peeled and finely diced
- 1 tablespoon fresh parsley, chopped
- ½ tablespoon fresh thyme, chopped
- ½ teaspoon paprika
- ½ teaspoon caraway seeds, crushed (optional)
- ½ teaspoon pink peppercorns, crushed (optional)
- 3 tablespoons all-purpose flour
- 1 tablespoon Dijon mustard
- 2 cups chicken stock, divided
- 1 cup mustard greens, thinly sliced
- 1 cup Swiss cheese, freshly shredded
- 2 cups corned beef, medium diced or shredded
- Kosher salt, to taste
- 2 sheets frozen puff pastry, thawed
- 1 egg, beaten
- ½ tablespoon flaky salt, for garnish
- Items Needed:
- 4 ramekins (8–10 ounces each)
- Rolling pin
- Pastry brush

Directions:

1. Melt the butter in a medium saucepan over medium-high heat. Stir in the fennel, garlic, potatoes, and carrot and cook for 1 minute, until fragrant.
2. Whisk in the parsley, thyme, paprika, caraway seeds, pink peppercorns, and flour and cook for 1 minute, stirring constantly.
3. Add the Dijon mustard and whisk to combine, followed immediately by 1 cup of the chicken stock, constantly whisking as the sauce thickens, then stir in the mustard greens.
4. Add the rest of the stock, then lower the heat to medium-low and simmer for 5 minutes.
5. Stir in the Swiss cheese and corned beef, then season to taste with kosher salt.
6. Fill each of the ramekins with the corned beef and vegetable mixture.
7. Roll out the puff pastry sheets and cut out 4 circles, each approximately ½-inch larger in diameter than the ramekins. Place the puff pastry circles onto the ramekins and seal the edges around the top.
8. Brush the tops of the puff pastries with a thin layer of the beaten egg and sprinkle with a pinch of flaky salt.
9. Place the crisper plate into the Smart Air Fryer basket.

10. Select the Preheat function, adjust temperature to 375°F, then press Start/Pause.
11. Place 2 of the ramekins onto the crisper plate. You will need to work in batches.
12. Set temperature to 375°F and time to 9 minutes, then press Start/Pause.
13. Remove the mini pot pies when done, then serve.

Leek & Mushroom Pie

Ingredients:
- 300g/2 leeks
- 500g mushrooms
- 3 Cloves garlic
- 1 Tbsp corn flour
- 125ml vegetable stock
- 2 Tbsp Dijon
- 250ml oatly cream
- 5g fresh thyme
- Vegan milk, for brushing the pastry
- 1 roll frozen puff pastry, defrosted (vegan friendly)

Directions:
1. Thinly slice the leeks and mushrooms. Using sauté on your Instant Pot or a frying pan, cook the leeks until just starting to soften, then add the mushrooms. Cook until the mushrooms are soft and browned. Add the garlic and cook for 1 more minute.
2. Mix the corn flour with a little vegetable stock to form a smooth slurry, then pour the cornflour mixture, remaining tock and oatly cream into the sautéed vegetables and cook until thickened. Pick the thyme from the woody stems and add this to the pie filling. Mix in the Dijon, and season to taste with salt and pepper.
3. Spoon the filling into a suitable size dish to fit in your Instant Vortex. An 18cm pie dish is perfect and allows plenty of room for the air to circulate and ensure the pie cooks evenly. Unroll your defrosted pastry, then cut a circle big enough to cover your pie. Place your pastry circle on top of your filling and crimp the edges to the pie dish to seal everything together. Poke a few small holes in the centre of the pie to allow the steam to escape, then brush the pastry with a little oat milk,
4. Place the pie into the basket of your air fryer. Select Air Fry, set the time to 25 minutes and the temperature to 170°C. Cook the pie until the pastry is beautifully puffed and crisp. Once cooked, remove the pie from the Vortex and serve immediately alongside your sides of choice.

Air Fryer Blueberry Muffins

Servings: 12
Cooking Time: 10 Minutes

Ingredients:
- 62ml (1/4 cup) vegetable oil
- 125 ml (1/2 cup) castor sugar
- 1 egg
- 125ml plain yogurt
- 5ml vanilla essence
- 250 ml (1 cup) cake flour
- 7ml (1 ½ tsp) baking powder
- Pinch salt
- 125 ml fresh or frozen blueberries
- Zest 1 lemon (optional)
- Topping:
- zest 2 lemon
- ½ cup castor sugar

Directions:
1. Whisk together the oil & castor sugar.
2. Add the egg, yogurt and vanilla essence and mix well.
3. Sift the flour, baking powder & salt together.
4. Fold the wet ingredients into the flour mix until the mixture just comes together.
5. Add the blueberries and lemon zest and fold to incorporate – do not over mix.
6. Spoon the mixture into 12 silicone cupcake molds.
7. For topping mix the castor sugar and lemon zest together and sprinkle on top of muffins.

8. Set the Instant Vortex (or Duo Crisp) to Bake at 180c for 10 mins, it will Pre Heat to the required temperature.
9. Once Vortex (or Duo Crisp) beeps "add food", it has reached temperature so place the muffins in the drawer.
10. You may need to cook the muffins in two batches depending on the size of your muffin molds.
11. Check after 10 mins.
12. Allow to cool and enjoy!

Salted Caramel Snickerdoodle Skillet Cookie

Servings: 4

Ingredients:
- 2¾ cups all-purpose flour
- 2 teaspoons cream of tartar
- 1 teaspoon baking soda
- ½ teaspoon kosher salt
- 1 teaspoon ground cinnamon, plus more for serving
- 1½ cups granulated sugar
- 4 ounces unsalted butter, room temperature
- 1 teaspoon vanilla extract
- 2 large eggs
- ½ cup salted caramel, plus more for serving
- Vanilla ice cream, for serving
- Items Needed:
- Stand mixer fitted with paddle attachment
- Cast iron skillet (6-inch diameter) or cake pan

Directions:
1. Whisk the flour, cream of tartar, baking soda, salt, and cinnamon together in a medium bowl.
2. Cream the sugar and butter together in a stand mixer fitted with the paddle attachment, then add the vanilla extract.
3. Add the eggs, one at a time, until fully combined, scraping down the sides of the bowl as needed with a rubber spatula.
4. Add the dry ingredients to the stand mixer and beat on low just until combined. Add

the salted caramel and stir to swirl it into the dough, but do not mix it in completely.
5. Fill the skillet or cake pan ⅔ full with dough. Reserve the remaining dough in the refrigerator for a second batch of cookies later.
6. Place the cooking pot into the base of the Indoor Grill, followed by the basket.
7. Select the Bake function, adjust temperature to 320°F and time to 20 minutes, then press Start/Pause to preheat.
8. Place the skillet or cake pan into the preheated basket, then close the lid.
9. Select the Broil function, adjust time 3 minutes, then press Start/Pause.
10. Remove the skillet or cake pan when done and let cool slightly.
11. Serve the cookie in slices, drizzled with salted caramel sauce, sprinkled with cinnamon, and a scoop of vanilla ice cream on top.

Homemade Cannoli

Servings: 20

Ingredients:
- FOR THE FILLING:
- 1 (16-oz.) container ricotta
- 1/2 c. mascarpone cheese
- 1/2 c. powdered sugar, divided
- 3/4 c. heavy cream
- 1 tsp. pure vanilla extract
- 1 tsp. orange zest
- 1/4 tsp. kosher salt
- 1/2 c. mini chocolate chips, for garnish
- FOR THE SHELLS:
- 2 c. all-purpose flour, plus more for surface
- 1/4 c. granulated sugar
- 1 tsp. kosher salt
- 1/2 tsp. cinnamon
- 4 tbsp. cold butter, cut into cubes
- 6 tbsp. white wine
- 1 large egg
- 1 egg white, for brushing
- Vegetable oil, for frying

Directions:

1. MAKE FILLING:
2. Drain ricotta by placing it a fine mesh strainer set over a large bowl. Let drain in refrigerator for at least an hour and up to overnight.
3. In a large bowl using a hand mixer, beat heavy cream and 1/4 cup powdered sugar until stiff peaks form.
4. In another large bowl, combine ricotta, mascarpone, remaining 1/4 cup powdered sugar, vanilla, orange zest, and salt. Fold in whipped cream. Refrigerate until ready to fill cannoli, at least 1 hour.
5. MAKE SHELLS:
6. In a large bowl, whisk together flour, sugar, salt, and cinnamon. Cut butter into flour mixture with your hands or pastry cutter until pea-sized. Add wine and egg and mix until a dough forms. Knead a few times in bowl to help dough come together. Pat into a flat circle, then wrap in plastic wrap and refrigerate at least 1 hour and up to overnight.
7. On a lightly floured surface, divide dough in half. Roll one half out to ⅛" thick. Use a 4" circle cookie cutter to cut out dough. Repeat with remaining dough. Re-roll scraps to cut a few extra circles.
8. Wrap dough around cannoli molds and brush egg whites where the dough will meet to seal together.
9. FOR FRYING:
10. In a large pot over medium heat, heat about 2" of oil to 360°. Working in batches, add cannoli molds to oil and fry, turning occasionally, until golden, about 4 minutes. Remove from oil and place on a paper towel-lined plate. Let cool slightly.
11. When cool enough to handle or using a kitchen towel to hold, gently twist shells off of molds to remove.
12. Place filling in a pastry bag fitted with an open star tip. Pipe filling into shells, then dip ends in mini chocolate chips.
13. FOR AIR FRYER:
14. Working in batches, place molds in basket of air fryer and cook at 350° for 12 minutes, or until golden.
15. When cool enough to handle or using a kitchen towel to hold, gently remove twist shells off of molds.
16. Place filling in a pastry bag fitted with an open star tip. Pipe filling into shells, then dip ends in mini chocolate chips.

Frosty Snowman Brownie Cupcakes

Servings: 24
Cooking Time: 22-25 Minutes

Ingredients:

- Cupcakes:
- 310 grams bittersweet chocolate
- 310 grams unsalted butter
- 370 grams eggs, whisked
- 1 pound   granulated sugar
- ½ tablespoon vanilla
- 40 grams unsweetened dark chocolate cocoa powder
- 40 grams unsweetened cocoa powder
- 225 grams all-purpose flour
- Items Needed:
- Large heatproof bowl
- Kitchen scale
- Stand mixer
- Cake testers, skewers, or toothpicks
- 24 paper cupcake liners
- Snowman Faces:
- 2 tablespoons powdered sugar
- 1 cup heavy cream
- 4 cups sweetened desiccated   coconut, plus more as needed
- 1 cup sanding sugar, plus more as needed
- 2 packs Sour Punch® straws, cut into 1½-inch pieces (1 pack red, 1 pack green), for earmuffs
- 48 circular gummy candies, for earmuffs
- 5 pieces dried apricots, cut into triangles, for noses
- 48 pieces of mini semi-sweet chocolate chips, for eyes

- 5 rolls of Smarties®, red and pink ones separated, for cheeks
- 1 pack sour streamers/belts, for smile

Directions:
1. Cupcakes:
2. Combine the chocolate and butter into a large heatproof bowl. Set up a double boiler station on the stove by simmering a pot of water and placing the bowl over it.
3. Melt the chocolate and butter over the double boiler and remove from heat, about 8 minutes.
4. Place the eggs, sugar, and vanilla into the stand mixer bowl. Mix on high speed for 8 minutes to yield a thick and glossy mixture, then lower speed to low.
5. Stream the warm, melted chocolate into the rotating stand mixer to temper the egg mixture. Once all the chocolate is added to the stand mixer, adjust speed to medium and whisk for another 5 minutes.
6. Whisk the flour and cocoa powders together in a medium bowl, then gently fold it into the wet batter.
7. Select the Preheat function on the Air Fryer, adjust temperature to 320°F, and press Start/Pause.
8. Fill each cupcake liner ¾ full with 3 ounces of batter.
9. Place 9 cupcakes into the preheated inner basket. You will need to work in batches.
10. Set temperature to 320°F and time to 20 minutes, then press Start/Pause.
11. Remove when done.
12. Note: Check the doneness of the cupcakes. If a cake tester comes out clean, it is ready to cool. If batter still comes out on the tester, bake an additional 2-3 minutes.
13. Cool completely on a wire rack and set aside.
14. Snowman Faces:
15. Place the powdered sugar and heavy cream into the stand mixer bowl and whip until stiff peaks form to make the whipped cream.
16. Spread 1 to 2 tablespoons of whipped cream over the top of each cooled cupcake.
17. Dip the cupcakes into the coconut, then sprinkle the tops with sanding sugar.
18. Bend the Sour Punch® straws so they are curved into an arched wide "U" shape.
19. Place 1 curved "U" shaped Sour Punch® straw piece upside down onto the very top of each cupcake. Then, place 2 gummy candies on each end of the upside down "U" to form the candy earmuffs.
20. Position the apricot triangles in the top-center of each cupcake to form the snowman's nose.
21. Place 2 mini chocolate chips above the nose to form the snowman's eyes, with the tip of the chocolate chip pressed into the coconut.
22. Add 2 pink or red Smarties® onto each cupcake to form the snowman's rosy cheeks.
23. Cut a small strip of a sour streamer to form the snowman's smile.
24. Serve your snowmen immediately.

Roast Dinner Yorkshire Pudding Wraps

Ingredients:
- 1 x 20cm/8" cake tin
- 90g flour
- 1 pinch salt
- 20ml water
- 2 eggs
- 80ml full fat milk
- 2g fresh chives, thinly sliced
- Oil for the tin
- Serving Suggestions:
- Roast beef, horseradish, roast potatoes (reheated until crisp), leftover green veg (we used Brussel sprouts, and sautéed greens). Add mustard if desired.
- Sautéed mushrooms or nut roast, Vortex crispy chickpeas (lightly oiled, Air Fry on 205°C for 6 mins), roast potatoes, roasted butternut, sauce of choice (a plant based white sauce, or salsa verde is lovely here!)
- Roast Chicken, stuffing, gravy, cauliflower cheese, honey roasted carrots broccoli – All

reheated in the Vortex Air Fryer (Grill on 205°C for 4 mins)

- Roast Lamb, Mint sauce, minted peas, mixed roasted veggies, rosemary roast potatoes
- No Roast leftovers? No problem!
- Cook some sausages and serve with mustard mayo (1Tbso Dijon +2 Tbsp Mayo) and buttery sautéed cabbage

Directions:
1. Add the flour and salt in a bowl and make a well in the middle. Add the water, eggs and milk and whisk the batter until no lumps remain. Then mix in the chives. Place the batter into the fridge to rest for as long as you can. Resting the batter is an important step as this will yield ever loftier results the longer the batter sits. 30 minutes before you are ready to cook, remove the batter from the fridge and allow it to come back to room temperature. Gather your roast dinner fillings, and reheat them as needed in the air fryer then set aside to keep warm while you cook the yorkshire pudding wraps.
2. Drizzle your sponge tin with oil until it covers the base of the tin in a 1mm layer. Place the oiled tin into the basket of the Instant Vortex Air Fryer. Select Air Fry, set the temperature to 205°C and the time to 8 minutes. Press Start and allow the air fryer to preheat with the cake tin inside. When prompted, open the drawer and pour exactly half of your batter into the heated cake tin.
3. Cook the Yorkshire pudding until deeply golden and puffy (ignore when prompted to turn food.) Once cooked remove the hot Yorkshire pudding wrap from the cake tin with tongs, then set aside to keep warm. Add in a little more oil into the cake tin, then repeat the cooking process with the remaining batter.
4. Once both pudding wraps are cooked, load them up with your favourite leftovers, roll up and serve immediately.

Tips for the puffiest pudding:
Rest time: The single most important step. Resting the batter will increase the rise of the puddings, and lead to a tastier and more complex final flavour. Aim for a few hours minimum if you can, or let them sit for up to three days for gravity defying pudding. Warm vs cold batter: A personal choice. Room temperature batter will yield tall, crispy puddings with a hollow core. Cold batter will create denser puddings with a pronounced cup. Preheat your cake tin and oil for a great puff.

How To Cook Patty Pan Squash
Servings: 6
Cooking Time: 10 Minutes
Ingredients:
- BASIC PATTY PAN SQUASH:
- 2 lb Patty pan squash (cut into pieces of the same size; you can cut them in half, or into quarters or wedges if they are larger)
- 2 tbsp Olive oil
- 1 tsp Sea salt
- 1/2 tsp Black pepper
- OPTIONAL FLAVOR BOOSTERS:
- 2 tsp Italian seasoning
- 1 tsp Garlic powder
- 1/2 tsp Crushed red pepper flakes

Directions:
1. SAUTEED PATTYPAN SQUASH:
2. Heat the olive oil in a large skillet over medium-high heat.
3. Add the pattypans and arrange, cut side down, in a single layer. Season with salt, pepper, and any flavor boosters, if using. (Work in batches if they don't fit in a single layer.)
4. Sear the squash for 3-5 minutes, without moving, until golden on the bottom. Flip and repeat until golden on the other side.
5. ROASTED PATTYPAN SQUASH:
6. Preheat the oven to 450 degrees F (232 degrees C).

7. In a large bowl, toss the pattypan squash with olive oil, salt, pepper, and any flavor boosters, if using.
8. Transfer the squash to a baking sheet and arrange, cut side down, in a single layer.
9. Roast pattypan squash for 15-20 minutes until tender and golden brown on the bottom. (If desired, you can stir halfway through for more even browning.)
10. GRILLED PATTYPAN SQUASH:
11. Preheat the outdoor grill for at least 10 minutes, or a grill pan on the stovetop, over medium-high heat.
12. In a large bowl, toss the pattypan squash with olive oil, salt, pepper, and any flavor boosters, if using. (If using an outdoor grill, larger squash pieces work best, so they won't fall through the grates.)
13. Place the squash, cut side down, onto the grill or grill pan in a single layer.
14. Grill for 3-4 minutes, until the grill marks form on the bottom. Flip and grill for 3-4 more minutes on the other side, until the squash is tender.
15. AIR FRYER PATTYPAN SQUASH:
16. In a large bowl, toss the pattypan squash with olive oil, salt, pepper, and any flavor boosters, if using.
17. Place the pattypan squash in the air fryer basket, cut side down, in a single layer. (Cook in batches if they don't all fit in a single layer.)
18. Air fry for 10-12 minutes at 400 degrees F (204 degrees C), until crispy and golden.

Air Fryer Berry Crisp

Servings: 2

Ingredients:
- FRUIT FILLING
- 1 c. fresh raspberries
- 3/4 c. fresh blueberries
- 1/2 c. fresh blackberries
- 2 tbsp. granulated sugar
- 2 tsp. ground flaxseeds
- 1/2 tsp. pure vanilla extract

- Pinch of kosher salt
- TOPPING
- 1/3 c. whole wheat flour
- 3 tbsp. old-fashioned rolled oats or chopped nuts, such as almonds or pecans
- 1 tbsp. granulated sugar
- Pinch of kosher salt
- 2 tbsp. butter, softened
- Olive oil cooking spray

Directions:
1. FRUIT FILLING
2. In a medium bowl, toss raspberries, blueberries, blackberries, sugar, flaxseeds, vanilla, and salt until coated.
3. Divide berry mixture between 2 (6") aluminum pie plates.

TOPPING

In a medium bowl, whisk flour, oats, sugar, and salt. Add butter and, using your hands, squeeze mixture together until clumps form.

Sprinkle topping over filling; generously spray with cooking spray. Place 1 pan in an air-fryer basket. Cook at 370° until filling is bubbly and top is golden, about 15 minutes. Let cool slightly. Repeat with remaining crisp.

Air Fryer Crab Cakes

Servings: 4
Cooking Time: 10 Minutes

Ingredients:
- 1 large egg whisked
- 1 1/2 tablespoons mayonnaise
- 1/2 teaspoon Dijon mustard
- 1 teaspoon Worcestershire sauce
- 1 teaspoon Old bay seasoning
- 1/4 teaspoon salt
- 1/4 teaspoon pepper
- 1/4 stalk celery finely chopped
- 2 tablespoons parsley finely chopped
- 1/4 small bell pepper finely chopped
- 1/2 lb crab meat canned or fresh
- 1/3 cup panko bread crumbs

Directions:

1. Add all the ingredients, except for the bread crumbs, until combined. Fold through the bread crumbs at the end.
2. Form the mixture into eight crab cakes and place them on a plate lined with parchment paper. Freeze the plate for 5 minutes.
3. Preheat the air fryer to 200C/400F.
4. Grease the air fryer basket and place four crab cakes in it. Air fry for 7-8 minutes, flipping halfway through.
5. Repeat the process until all the crab cakes are cooked.

Notes

TO STORE: In airtight food containers, you can refrigerate leftover crab cakes for up to 5 days.

TO FREEZE: Using freezer-safe bags/ containers and parchment paper, you can freeze them for up to 1 month.

TO REHEAT: Preheat the air fryer to 400°F before putting in the crab cakes. 2 to 3 minutes is enough to reheat them thoroughly.

Air Fryer Caramel Rolls

Servings: 5

Ingredients:
- 1 can (17.5 oz) refrigerated Pillsbury™ Grands!™ Cinnamon Rolls with Original Icing (5 Count)
- 1/2 cup caramel dessert sauce, room temperature
- 1/3 cup chopped pecans

Directions:
1. Cut two 8-inch rounds of cooking parchment paper. Place one round in bottom of air fryer basket. Spray with cooking spray.
2. Separate dough into 5 rolls; set icing aside. Place 3 rolls on parchment paper in air fryer basket, spacing apart. Cover remaining rolls with plastic wrap, and refrigerate.
3. Set air fryer to 320°F; cook 12 minutes. Place a large plate over air fryer basket, and invert. Discard parchment. Carefully transfer cinnamon rolls back to air fryer,

bottom side up. Cook 2 to 4 minutes or until golden brown and rolls are cooked through. Remove from air fryer; cover loosely with foil to keep warm while cooking second batch. Repeat for remaining 2 rolls, and place on remaining parchment round in basket of air fryer. Cook as directed above.
4. Meanwhile, in small bowl, mix caramel sauce and pecans. Spread 1 teaspoon reserved icing on top of each baked roll. Top with caramel mixture. Serve warm. Serve with remaining icing.

Vortex Air Fryer Apple Cheddar Stuffed Chicken Breast

Servings: 2
Cooking Time: 25 Minutes

Ingredients:
- 2 boneless skinless chicken breasts 5-6 oz each, flattened to ¼ inch
- ½ cup apple peeled and diced
- ¼ cup cheddar cheese shredded
- 1 tablespoon bread crumbs
- salt and pepper to taste

Directions:
1. Preheat the air fryer to 350°F.
2. In a small bowl combine the apple, cheese and bread crumbs. Mix until fully combined.
3. Flatten the chicken to 1/4-inch thick and season with salt and pepper.
4. Spread half of the apple mixture into the center of the chicken breast and roll up. Secure with toothpicks.
5. Spray the chicken with cooking spray or brush with oil and season to taste with salt & pepper.
6. Place the chicken breasts in the air fryer basket and cook for 20-25 minutes or until the chicken reaches 165°F internally.

Blueberry Pie Bars

Ingredients:
- Crust and Topping
- 3/4 cups all purpose flour
- 1/4 cup sugar
- pinch salt
- 6 Tbsp. cold butter, cut into cubes
- Filling
- 1 egg
- 1/2 cup sugar
- 2 Tbsp. + 2 tsp all purpose flour
- 1/4 cup sour cream
- pinch salt
- 1.5 cups fresh blueberries

Directions:
1. To make the crust, mix the flour, sugar, salt and cubed butter to mixing bowl, beat until combined and crumbly. Do not overmix.
2. Reserve 1/2 cup of mixture and set aside.
3. Spray an 8x8 glass baking dish with non stick spray. Firmly press the crust mixture into your pan, covering the bottom.
4. Bake crust at 350F for 10-12 minutes.
5. While crust is baking- whisk the egg in a large bowl. Add sugar, flour, sour cream, salt and gently fold in the blueberries.
6. When crust is ready, remove from oven and spoon filling over the top of the crust.
7. Sprinkle the top with remaining crust mixture you had set aside, distributing evenly.
8. Bake at 350F for 45 minutes.
9. Cool for at least 10 minutes before serving. Enjoy!

Air Fryer Cream Cheese Cherry Pies

Servings: 4
Cooking Time: 6 Minutes

Ingredients:
- 12 ounces cherry pie filling
- 8 ounces cream cheese softened
- 1 egg beaten
- 1 pie crust rolled refrigerated dough

Directions:
1. Roll out the refrigerated pie dough on a cutting board and cut them into 6" dough circles.
2. Use a mini pie maker, round cookie cutter or a small plate as a template for the desired size.
3. In a medium-sized bowl mix the cherry pie filling and cream cheese together.
4. Whisk the egg in a separate shallow bowl.
5. Scoop 2 tablespoons of the cherry cream cheese mixture into the center of the dough circles.
6. Fold the circle in half, then use a fork to crimp the edges.
7. Spritz the air fryer basket with cooking spray.
8. Place pies in a single layer into the prepared air fryer basket, then brush each pie with the egg mixture.
9. Air fry the pies at 380 degrees F for 6 minutes, flipping the pies carefully halfway through the cooking process.
10. Remove pies and place them on baking racks so the pies remain crispy prior to serving.
11. Serve while warm.

NOTES

Optional Flavors: Vanilla extract, nutmeg, lemon zest, cinnamon, cardamom, almond extract or all spice.

Optional Toppings: Powdered sugar, granulated sugar, caramel sauce, cinnamon sugar, toasted coconut or a dollop of whipped cream.

Kitchen Tips: Use parchment paper liners if you do not have nonstick cooking spray.

NOTE: I make this recipe in my Cosori 5.8 qt. air fryer. Depending on your air fryer, size and wattages, the cook time may need to be adjusted 1-2 minutes.

Change things up!There are several flavors of canned filling that are available in your local grocery stores that you can use in this recipe. Some popular flavors are apple, raspberry, peach, strawberry and blueberry.

Chocolate Chickpea Bites

Ingredients:
- 1 can of chickpeas (you can also use your Instant Pot to cook them from scratch)
- 1 tbsp cooking oil
- 1 slab dark chocolate of choice

Directions:
1. Heat your Vortex air fryer to 200°C and set the timer to 15 minutes.
2. Drain and rinse chickpeas. To get rid of excessive moisture, you can pat-dry using a paper towel.
3. Toss the chickpeas with your cooking oil of choice.
4. Dump the chickpeas in your Vortex air fryer drawer. Cook for 12-15 minutes, shaking a couple of times. When chickpeas are cooked to your liking, remove from air fryer and let them cool.
5. Melt your chocolate and add all of your chickpeas. Make sure they're all evenly coated with chocolate and spread them out on some baking paper.
6. Once set, enjoy!

Air Fryer Halloween Ghost Cupcakes

Servings: 24
Cooking Time: 30 Minutes

Ingredients:
- cake mix 15.25 oz
- 1 1/4 cups water
- 1/2 cup vegetable oil
- Topping
- 1 tub frosting
- 1 package candy eyes

Directions:
1. Air fry 350 degrees Fahrenheit 10-12 minutes. Makes 2 dozen cupcakes
2. Use a medium bowl, to combine the cake mix with water, vegetable oil, and eggs. (or according to your box mix directions) Stir, or if using an electric mixer, beat on medium speed until creamy.
3. Once the batter is prepared, place the silicone liners in your air fryer basket.
4. Carefully pour the cupcake batter from the mixing bowl until they are about ¾ full.
(You can use a cupcake tin with liners, if it will fit in your air fryer)
5. Air fry the cupcakes at 350 degrees Fahrenheit for 10-12 minutes.
6. Once done, remove from the air fryer basket and start the next batch. Be sure to allow the cupcakes to cool before frosting.
7. To top the cupcakes with your ghost frosting, add vanilla or buttercream on cupcake using a frosting bag. Going in a continual circular motion, continue to make a full circle, until you have a small mound of frosting, to create a ghost form.
8. Add the two edible eyes to each ghost to complete the face.

NOTES
Not all Air fryers are the same. Wattages can affect cooking time.
Having cake batter near the air fryer fan can blow the tops of the cupcakes just a bit.
Be careful not to fill the silicone liners to full or the batter will blow around in the air fryer.
If you can't find candy eyeballs, you can use black writing icing, a drop of black food gel, or mini chocolate chips for the eyes.

Grammy's Jam Thumbprints

Ingredients:
- 2/3 cup butter
- 1/3 cup sugar
- 2 eggs (yolks separated; whites saved)
- 1 tsp vanilla
- ½ tsp salt
- 1 ½ cup flour
- Walnuts, chopped
- Strawberry preserves

Directions:
1. Cream butter and sugar until fluffy
2. Add in yolks, vanilla, and salt – beat well.
3. Gradually add in flour.
4. Shape into ¾ inch balls. Dip into beaten egg whites. Then roll in finely chopped walnuts.
5. Place on greased cookies sheet. Press down in center with thumb.
6. Bake in your Air Fryer Oven at 350*F for 10-12 minutes. Let cool.
7. Add strawberry preserves into the thumbprint.

POULTRY RECIPES

Air Fryer Chicken Fajitas

Servings: 4
Cooking Time: 10 Minutes

Ingredients:

- 1/2 pound boneless and skinless chicken breasts, cut into 1/2-inch wide strips
- 1 large red or yellow bell pepper, cut into strips
- 1 medium red onion, cut into strips
- 1 tablespoon olive oil
- 1 tablespoon chili powder
- 2 teaspoons lime juice
- 1 teaspoon cumin
- Salt and pepper to taste
- OPTIONAL
- pinch of cayenne pepper
- tortillas for serving

Directions:

1. Preheat your air fryer to 370 degrees.
2. Put the chicken strips, bell pepper, onion, oil, chili powder, lime juice, cumin, salt and pepper, and cayenne pepper (if using) in a bowl and mix.
3. Place the chicken fajitas in the air fryer and cook for 10-13 minutes, shaking the basket halfway through. The fajitas are done when the chicken hits 165 degrees F at its thickest point.
4. Remove the fajitas from the air fryer, warm tortillas if needed, and enjoy!

NOTES

How to Reheat Chicken Fajitas in an Air Fryer: Preheat your air fryer to 350 degrees.

Cook chicken fajitas for 3-5 minutes until heated thoroughly and enjoy!

How to Warm Tortillas in the Air Fryer:

Cover tortillas with aluminum foil and cook for 5-10 minutes in a preheated air fryer at 370 degrees.

Air Fryer General Tso's Chicken

Servings: 4
Cooking Time: 10 Minutes

Ingredients:

- 1 lb chicken breast boneless, skinless chicken breast or thighs, cut into 1-2 inch pieces
- 1 tbsp cornstarch
- ½ tsp salt
- ¼ tsp black pepper
- ¼ cup General Tso's Sauce
- Garnish: Chopped green onions, sesame seeds
- Homemade General Tso's Sauce:
- ⅓ cup rice wine or vinegar
- ¼ cup hoisin or teriyaki sauce
- 1 tsp red pepper flakes
- 1 tsp fresh garlic minced
- 1 tsp fresh ginger grated
- 1 tbsp granuated sugar
- 2 tbsp cornstarch

Directions:

1. In a medium shallow bowl, toss chicken pieces with cornstarch, salt and pepper, on both sides.
2. Place into the air fryer basket, that is lightly sprayed with nonstick spray.
3. Air fry at 380 degrees F for 8-10 minutes, tossing chicken halfway through cooking time. Chicken should be crispy and have an internal temperature of 165 degrees F.
4. Add sauce to chicken and toss in an air fryer basket. Return basket to air fryer and air fryer at 380 degrees F for 1-2 minutes. Serve with rice or broccoli.
5. To make Homemade General Tso's Sauce:
6. In a medium saucepan, add rice wine or vinegar, hoisin or teriyaki sauce, pepper flakes, garlic and ginger. Stir until fragrant.
7. Add in sugar, then stir together until sugar dissolves and sauce begins to lightly boil.
8. Remove from heat and add cornstarch.
9. Continue whisking until the sauce thickens.

NOTES
Variations
Use different sauce ingredients - While this air fryer general Tso's chicken recipe is perfect as is, you can always change the sauce and change the flavor. You can add spicy flavor with chili flakes or any other spicy sauce you like. Adding soy sauce is also a great way to add a different flavor.

Slow Cooker Honey Mustard Chicken Recipe

Servings: 6
Cooking Time: 4 Hours

Ingredients:
- 2 to 2.5 pounds (910g-1140g) boneless skinless chicken breasts or chicken thighs
- 1/2 cup (120ml) honey
- 1/4 cup (60ml) soy sauce (or Tamari for gluten free)
- 1/4 cup (60ml) mustard
- 2 Tablespoons (30ml) malt vinegar (or distilled vinegar for gluten free)
- 4 garlic cloves , mashed
- 1/2 teaspoon fresh ground black pepper , or to taste
- TO THICKEN THE SAUCE (OPTIONAL)
- 2 Tablespoons (30ml) cornstarch
- 2 Tablespoons (30ml) water

Directions:
1. In a 4 quart slow cooker, combine honey, soy sauce, mustard, malt vinegar, garlic and black pepper. Stir to combine all ingredients together well.
2. Add the chicken and press chicken down to cover it in as much sauce as possible.
3. Cook the chicken 4-5 hours on High or 6 hours on Low until the chicken is moist and tender.
4. Stir the chicken about 2 times, if possible, during the cooking and push the chicken down so it's immersed in the sauce.
5. Optional: to thicken the sauce (do this about 1 hour before chicken is finished cooking). Make the corn starch slurry: mix cornstarch and cold water in small bowl.

Stir the mixture so that all the cornstarch is completely dissolved, leaving no lumps.
6. Quickly stir in the cornstarch slurry into the crock pot teriyaki mixture and combine well so that the cornstarch doesn't thicken and become lumpy. Finish cooking for the final hour.
7. Serve the hot and delicious chicken over rice, pasta or in a sandwich!

Air Fryer Lemon Pepper Wings

Servings: 4
Cooking Time: 25 Minutes

Ingredients:
- 1 1/2 pounds chicken wings, drumettes and flats separated and tips discarded
- 2 teaspoons McCormick lemon pepper seasoning
- 1/4 teaspoon cayenne pepper
- FOR THE LEMON PEPPER SAUCE
- 3 tablespoons butter
- 1 teaspoon McCormicks lemon pepper seasoning
- 1 teaspoon honey

Directions:
1. Preheat your air fryer to 380 degrees.
2. Coat the chicken wings with lemon pepper seasoning and cayenne pepper.
3. Place the lemon pepper wings in the air fryer, filling it no more than halfway full. Cook for 20-22 minutes, shaking the basket halfway through cooking.
4. Increase the temperature to 400 degrees and cook for an additional 3-5 minutes to get a nice crispy skin on the chicken wings.
5. While the chicken wings are cooking, mix the melted butter, additional lemon pepper seasoning, and honey in a bowl.
6. Remove chicken wings from the air fryer and drizzle the lemon honey sauce on top. Enjoy!

Air Fryer Stuffing

Servings: 6
Cooking Time: 5 Minutes

Ingredients:

- 1 1/2 cups chicken broth
- 1 tsp sage
- 1/4 cup butter melted
- 1/2 cup celery, chopped about 2 stalks
- 1/4 cup onion, chopped about ½ small onion
- 4 cups herb seasoned breadcrumbs

Directions:

1. To make this recipe, begin by adding the bread crumbs into a medium bowl. Next, add in the broth and the melted butter. Stir together until the breadcrumbs and the liquids mix well.
2. Add in the chopped celery, onion, and sage. Stir together until the bread crumbs are well combined with the other ingredients. Transfer to an air fryer safe baking dish.
3. Place the stuffing in air fryer basket and air fry at 320 degrees F for 3-5 minutes cooking time.
4. Stir the stuffing halfway through cooking. Stuffing will be golden brown on top when done. Season with salt and black pepper as desired.

Air Fryer Chicken Thighs

Servings: 4
Cooking Time: 20 Minutes

Ingredients:

- 1 tablespoon paprika
- 1/2 tablespoon smoked paprika
- 2 teaspoons kosher salt
- 1 teaspoon garlic powder
- 1/2 teaspoon black pepper
- 4 bone-in, skin-on chicken thighs (about 2 to 2 1/2 pounds), see notes to use boneless chicken thighs
- 2 tablespoons extra virgin olive oil
- Lemon wedges for serving
- Chopped fresh parsley or cilantro for serving

Directions:

1. In a large bowl, combine the paprika, smoked paprika, salt, garlic powder, and black pepper.
2. Pat the chicken thighs very dry on both sides, then add to the bowl. Drizzle with the oil, then toss to coat in the spice mixture.
3. Preheat the air fryer to 400°F. Add the chicken thighs in a single layer, skin-side down (make sure they are not touching; if they are, cook the chicken in batches).
4. Air fry the chicken thighs for 16 to 22 minutes, flipping halfway through, until an instant read thermometer inserted at the thickest part of a thigh (but not touching bone) reaches 155°F. Set aside, cover, and let rest for 5 minutes (chicken is considered by the FDA cooked at 165°F, but the temperature will continue to rise as it rests; air fryer models differ in cooking time, so check early to be safe). Serve hot, with lemon wedges (squeeze them over the top of your serving) and sprinkled with fresh herbs.

Notes

FOR BONELESS THIGHS: Coat with the spice mixture as directed. Preheat the air fryer to 380°F, then add the chicken smooth-side down. Cook for 6 to 8 minutes, flipping halfway through, until the chicken reaches 155°F on an instant read thermometer. Let rest for 5 to 10 minutes (the temperature will continue to rise), then enjoy warm.

TO STORE: Refrigerate chicken in an airtight storage container for up to 4 days.

TO REHEAT: Gently rewarm leftovers in a baking dish in the oven at 350°F or in the microwave.

TO FREEZE: Freeze thighs in an airtight, freezer-safe storage container for up to 3 months. Let thaw overnight in the refrigerator before reheating.

Air Fryer Fried Chicken

Servings: 8
Cooking Time: 22 Minutes

Ingredients:

- 2 lb chicken pieces a mix of bone-in chicken thighs and drumsticks
- 1 cup buttermilk
- 1 teaspoon salt
- 1/2 teaspoon pepper
- For the breading
- 1 cup flour
- 1/2 cup cornstarch
- 1 teaspoon salt
- 1/2 teaspoon pepper
- 1 teaspoon smoked paprika

Directions:

1. Preheat the air fryer to 180C/350F.
2. In a mixing bowl, add the chicken, buttermilk, salt, and pepper, and let it sit for 10 minutes. In a separate bowl, whisk the breading mixture together.
3. Using tongs, pick up pieces of the chicken and shake off excess buttermilk. Moving quickly, dip the chicken in the breading on both sides.
4. Generously spray the air fryer basket. Place a single layer of chicken in it and generously spray it with cooking spray. Air fry the chicken for 15 minutes, flip, spray again, and cook for another 10 minutes.
5. Once the chicken reaches an internal temperature of 165F, they are ready to be removed from the air fryer. Repeat the process until all the chicken is cooked.

Notes
TO STORE: Use airtight containers to store the leftovers in the refrigerator for 3 days.
TO FREEZE: Put the cooked chicken in freezer-safe bags and freeze for up to 6 months.
TO REHEAT: You can reheat fried chicken in the air fryer or a preheated oven.

Peach Bbq Chicken

Ingredients:

- 2 lbs. chicken drumsticks
- 1 Tbsp olive oil
- Salt and pepper
- 1 Tbsp olive oil
- 2 Tbsp minced fresh garlic
- 2 Tbsp minced fresh ginger
- 1/4 cup orange juice
- 1 cup peach preserves
- 2 Tbsp apple cider vinegar
- 1/2 cup brown sugar
- 3 Tbsp brown mustard
- 1 Tbsp smoked paprika
- 2 tsp kosher salt
- 1/4 tsp red pepper flakes

Directions:

1. Preheat the air fryer oven to 400F.
2. Pat dry the drumsticks. Brush on some olive oil and season with salt and pepper on both sides.
3. Place on the baking pan accessory or the mesh rack accessory and cook for 10 minutes, flipping halfway.
4. Next make the Peach BBQ Sauce: Heat up 1 Tbsp. olive oil in a pan and add in the garlic and ginger paste. Cook for a couple of minutes.
5. Then add in the orange juice, peach preserves, apple cider vinegar, brown mustard, smoked paprika, salt and the red pepper flakes. Let that simmer for 10 minutes and set aside.
6. Remove the partially cooked chicken and baste on the Peach BBQ Sauce. Cook for another 10 minutes.
7. Once done, baste with more BBQ sauce. You can choose to eat them at this point or cook for an additional 3-5 minutes to crisp further.
8. Enjoy with any side of your choice!

Air Fryer Frozen Chicken Wings

Servings: 20

Cooking Time: 18 Minutes

Ingredients:

- 2 lb (1kg) frozen chicken wings pre-seasoned or breaded or frozen from fresh with no seasoning
- Seasoning for wings if not already seasoned
- Salt
- Black pepper
- Vegetable oil this will help the seasoning stick on the wings.

Directions:

1. Preheat the air fryer at 200C/400F for 3 to 5 minutes
2. Pre-seasoned wings instructions: add the frozen chicken wings in a single layer(it doesn't matter if they are touching).
3. Cook at 200C/400F for 10 minutes, remove the air fryer basket and flip the chicken and continue to cook for another 10 minutes. check on the chicken on this point to see if it is done to your liking otherwise, cook for an additional 5 minutes for the chicken to crisp up.
4. Serve and enjoy!
5. Instuctions for frozen wings not already seasoned:
6. If the chicken weren't already seasoned, spray cooking oil on the frozen chicken then season with salt and black pepper or any other seasoning of choice and cook at 200C/400F for 10 minutes, flip and cook for additional 10 to 15 minutes or until well done.
7. The internal temperature of cooked chicken should register 165F/73C

NOTES

How to store

Leftover cooked chicken wings can be stored in the fridge for up to 3 days in an airtight container. Make sure it is completely cooled before storing. Do not refreeze chicken the wings.

5 Ingredient Crispy Cheesy Air Fryer Chicken Dinner Recipe

Servings: 4

Cooking Time: 8 Minutes

Ingredients:

- 4 thin chicken breasts or two chicken breasts cut/pounded to be thin
- 1 cup milk
- [1/2 cup panko bread crumbs]
- 3/4-1 cup shaved Parmesan-Asiago cheese blend can use any type of hard shaved or shredded cheese like Parmesan, Asiago, Romano
- salt + pepper to taste

Directions:

1. Preheat your air fryer to 400 degrees. Spray the cooking basket lightly with cooking spray.
2. In a large bowl place the milk and chicken breasts. Sprinkle in a generous pinch of salt and freshly ground pepper. Allow to marinate in the milk for 10 minutes.
3. In a shallow bowl combine panko bread crumbs and shaved cheese.
4. Dredge chicken breasts through panko and cheese mixture (press the mixture on top of the chicken generously) and place in the air fryer basket. Make sure that the basket is not overcrowded. I fit 2 chicken breasts in the basket, so I did this in two batches. Spray the top of the chicken lightly with cooking spray (this 'locks on' the cheesy bread crumb topping).
5. Cook for 8 minutes, flipping the chicken breasts halfway through.
6. Remove from the air fryer, repeat the process with any remaining chicken breasts. If you want to warm everything, you can add the already cooked chicken breasts into the basket and cook them for 1 minute to warm them! Enjoy

Crispy Sesame Fried Chicken Recipe

Ingredients:
- 90g chicken breast strips
- 40g rolled porridge oats
- 25g self-raising flour
- 10g toasted sesame seeds
- ½ tbsp chicken bouillon powder
- 1 ½ tsp salt
- ½ tsp garlic powder
- ½ tsp onion powder
- ½ tsp soy sauce
- ¼ tsp dried basil
- ¼ tsp dried oregano
- ¼ tsp ground black pepper
- 60ml chicken stock

Directions:
1. Coat the chicken with ½ tsp salt, black pepper, and garlic and then chill for approximately 4 hours.
2. In a medium bowl, mix together the oats, sesame seeds, ½ tsp salt and chicken bouillon powder and set aside.
3. In a second bowl, combine the flour, ½ tsp salt, onion powder, basil, oregano, soy sauce, and chicken stock.
4. Dip the chicken into the stock mixture, then roll in the sesame seed mixture.
5. In a 200°C air fryer, add the chicken and cook for 15-20 minutes until golden brown and the chicken is cooked through.

Air Fryer Chicken Stuffed With Prosciutto And Fontina

Servings: 2
Cooking Time: 25 Minutes

Ingredients:
- 2 skinless boneless chicken breast halves
- 4 ounces fontina cheese, rind removed, cut into 2-inch sticks
- 2 slices prosciutto
- salt, to taste
- freshly ground black pepper, to taste
- 4 tablespoons unsalted butter
- 2 tablespoons extra-virgin olive oil
- 1 cup portobello mushrooms, sliced
- 1/2 cup dry white wine
- 3 sprigs rosemary
- 1 bunch baby arugula
- 1/2 lemon, juiced

Directions:
1. Place chicken breast halves between sheets of wax paper, and using a mallet or rolling pin, pound thin.
2. Wrap each fontina cheese stick with one slice prosciutto and place in center of each flattened chicken breast half. Roll chicken around prosciutto and cheese and secure with toothpicks or butcher's twine. Season chicken rolls with salt and black pepper.
3. In a heavy skillet, heat 2 tablespoons of the butter and 1 tablespoon of the olive oil. Quickly brown chicken rolls over medium heat, 2 to 3 minutes per side. Place chicken rolls in air fryer basket. Set air fryer temperature to 350 degrees, and air fry for 7 minutes. Remove chicken rolls to a cutting board and let rest for 5 minutes. Cut rolls at an angle into 6 slices.
4. Reheat skillet, add remaining butter, mushrooms, wine, and rosemary; season with salt and black pepper; and simmer for 10 minutes.
5. In a large bowl, toss arugula leaves in remaining olive oil, lemon juice, salt, and pepper. To serve, arrange chicken and mushrooms on bed of dressed arugula.

Homemade Air Fryer Chicken Nuggets

Servings: 4
Cooking Time: 8 Minutes

Ingredients:
- cooking/oil spray
- 2 chicken breasts cut into 1″ to 1.5″ cubes
- 1/3 cup olive oil more if needed
- 1.5 cup panko
- 1/4 cup parmesan
- 2 tsp sweet paprika

Directions:

1. Cut up your chicken breasts into 1″ to 5″ cubes and set them aside.
2. Set up your station with one bowl holding your olive oil, and the other holding your panko, parmesan, and paprika mix.
3. Spritz the inside of your air fryer lightly with some oil.
4. Dip your chicken cube into the olive oil, then place it into your coating. Make sure your nugget is well coated and place it into the air fryer. Repeat until your air fryer is full. Do not over crowd the air fryer, air fry in batches if needed.
5. Set your air fryer to 400F and cook your homemade chicken nuggets for 8 minutes.
6. Serve with your choice of dip.

Air Fryer Chicken Tenders Recipe

Servings: 4
Cooking Time: 20-48 Minutes

Ingredients:

- 1/4 cup well-shaken buttermilk or half-and-half
- 2 large eggs
- 2 cups panko breadcrumbs
- 2 teaspoons garlic powder
- 2 teaspoons onion powder
- 1 1/2 teaspoons kosher salt
- 1 1/2 teaspoons mustard powder
- 1/2 to 1 teaspoon freshly ground black pepper
- 1 1/2 pounds chicken tenders (10 to 12)
- 1/4 cup cornstarch
- Cooking spray

Directions:

1. Place 1/4 cup buttermilk or half-and-half and 2 large eggs in a medium bowl and whisk to combine. Place 2 cups panko breadcrumbs, 2 teaspoons garlic powder, 2 teaspoons onion powder, 1 1/2 teaspoons kosher salt, 1 1/2 teaspoons mustard powder, and 1/2 to 1 teaspoon black pepper in second bowl or shallow dish and whisk to combine.

2. Place 1/4 cup cornstarch on a rimmed baking sheet. Pat 1 1/2 pounds chicken tenders dry with paper towels. Place on the cornstarch and toss until fully coated. Working in batches, dip the chicken in the buttermilk mixture, then dredge in the panko mixture until fully coated. Return to the baking sheet in a single layer. Let rest at room temperature for 30 minutes, which gives the coating time to adhere to the chicken.

3. Heat an air fryer to 400°F. Coat both sides of the chicken with cooking spray. Working in batches as needed, arrange the chicken in a single layer in the air fryer basket. Air fry, flipping halfway through, until cooked through, golden-brown, and crispy, 10 to 12 minutes total. Serve with your favorite dipping sauce.

RECIPE NOTES

Storage: Refrigerate leftovers in an airtight container for up to 4 days. Reheat in a 350°F oven for 15 minutes or in an air fryer for 5 minutes.

Air Fryer Chicken Wings

Servings: 4
Cooking Time: 35 Minutes

Ingredients:

- 2 lb Chicken wings (flats and drumettes, either fresh or thawed from frozen)
- 1 tbsp Olive oil (optional)
- 2 tsp Baking powder
- 3/4 tsp Sea salt
- 1/4 tsp Black pepper

Directions:

1. Pat the chicken wings very dry with paper towels. (This will help them get crispy.)
2. In a large bowl, toss the wings with baking powder, olive oil (if using), sea salt and black pepper.
3. Place the chicken wings in the air fryer in a single layer, without touching too much. (Cook in batches if they don't fit.)

4. Air fry the chicken wings for 15 minutes at 250 degrees F. (If your wings are frozen, add an extra 10 minutes at this step.)
5. Flip the wings over. Increase the air fryer temperature to 430 degrees F (or the highest your air fryer goes). Air fry for about 15 to 20 minutes, until chicken wings are done and crispy.

Chicken Rollatini Stuffed With Zucchini And Mozzarella

Servings: 8
Cooking Time: 30 Minutes

Ingredients:
- 1 tsp olive oil
- 4 cloves garlic (chopped)
- 1 1/2 cups 1 medium zucchini, shredded
- 1/4 cup + 2 tbsp Romano cheese (or parmesan)
- 3 oz part skim shredded mozzarella
- salt and pepper to taste
- 8 thin chicken cutlets (3 oz each)
- 1/2 cup Italian seasoned breadcrumbs
- 1 lemon (juice of)
- 1 tbsp olive oil
- salt and fresh pepper
- olive oil non-stick spray

Directions:
1. Wash and dry cutlets, season with salt and pepper. Preheat oven to 450°. Lightly spray a baking dish with non-stick spray.
2. In a large skillet, heat oil on medium-high heat. When hot saute the garlic 1 minute, or until golden. Add zucchini, 1/4 cup Romano cheese, salt and pepper and saute about 3-4 minutes, stirring occasionally. Set aside to cool. When cool, add mozzarella cheese and mix to combine.
3. Lay chicken cutlets down on a working surface and spread 3 tbsp of zucchini-cheese mixture on each cutlet. Loosely roll each one and keep seam side down.
4. Combine breadcrumbs and remaining 2 tbsp of Romano cheese in one bowl; in a

second bowl combine olive oil, lemon juice, and pepper.
5. Dip chicken in lemon-oil mixture, then in breadcrumbs and place seam side down in a baking dish (no toothpicks needed). Repeat with the remaining chicken. When finished, lightly spray with oil spray.
6. Bake 25 - 30 minutes. Serve immediately. Serving size is listed as one, but if you are having this with a salad, I suggest you have two.

Air Fryer Directions:
Follow steps above 1 through 6.
Preheat the air fryer once again to 400F. Spray both sides of the chicken with oil. Cook, in two batches 12 minutes turning halfway.

Air Fryer Frozen Chicken Pot Pie

Servings: 2
Cooking Time: 24 Minutes

Ingredients:
- 2 frozen chicken pot pies
- salt and pepper to taste

Directions:
1. Preheat the air fryer to 360°F.
2. Place the chicken pot pies in the air fryer basket.
3. Cook for 20-24 minutes or until the crust is golden brown and the filling is warm.
4. Season as desired.

Air Fryer Chicken Nuggets

Servings: 4
Cooking Time: 12 Minutes

Ingredients:
- 2 large chicken breasts cut into nuggets
- 1 cup panko bread crumbs
- 1/3 cup parmesan cheese
- 1/2 teaspoon salt
- 1 tablespoon olive oil
- 1/2 cup all-purpose flour
- 3 large eggs lightly beaten

Directions:

1. Preheat the air fryer to 200C/400F.
2. In a mixing bowl, add the panko, parmesan cheese and salt, and oil, and mix until combined. In another bowl add the flour and in a third, add the beaten eggs.
3. Dip the chicken in the flour, shake off the excess, dip it in the egg, then coat with the panko mix, pressing firmly for it to stick on. Repeat the process until all the chicken is coated.
4. Generously grease the air fryer basket. In a single layer, add the chicken nuggets.
5. Spray the tops of the chicken nuggets and air fry for 12-15 minutes, or until golden and crispy.

Bbq Chicken Wings

Ingredients:
- 3 cm piece of fresh ginger, peeled and grated
- 1 garlic clove, crushed
- 3 tbsp orange marmalade
- 2 tbsp clear honey
- 1 tbsp sesame oil
- 2 tsp soy sauce
- 1 ½ tsp Chinese five-spice
- ½ tsp grated orange zest

Directions:
1. Mix all of the ingredients, except for the chicken wings, in a large bowl.
2. Dip the chicken wings into the mixture, cover and refrigerate for at least 2 hours or overnight, turning occasionally.
3. Plug in and switch on the air fryer at the mains power supply.
4. Set the temperature to 200°C and the time to approx. 15 mins and carefully place the chicken wings into the relevant cooking compartment.
5. Check that the chicken wings are cooked through before serving.
6. Serve immediately with your choice of sides.

Air Fryer Whole Chicken
Servings: 4
Cooking Time: 55 Minutes

Ingredients:
- 1 3- to 4-pound roasting chicken* giblets removed
- 2 1/2 teaspoons kosher salt divided
- 1 medium lemon cut into quarters
- 6 whole garlic cloves no need to peel
- 4 sprigs fresh thyme
- 2 tablespoons extra-virgin olive oil
- 1 teaspoon ground black pepper

Directions:
1. Remove the giblets from the chicken and pat very dry (no need to rinse). Season the inside of the chicken cavity with 1/2 teaspoon of the salt.
2. Stuff the chicken cavity with the lemon, garlic, and thyme.
3. Brush the outside of the chicken all over with the oil.
4. Sprinkle with the remaining 2 teaspoons salt and the black pepper.
5. Preheat the air fryer to 360 degrees F. Place the chicken in the air fryer breast-side down.
6. Air fry for 30 minutes, then slide out the basket and flip the chicken over.
7. Continue air frying until the chicken reaches 155 degrees on an instant read thermometer inserted in the thickest part of the breast, about 25 to 30 minutes more. Remove from the air fryer. Cover and let rest for at least 10 minutes before carving.

Notes

*Make sure your chicken fits in your air fryer basket without touching the heating element before you begin. I have a 5.5-quart air fryer and it holds a chicken that is between 3 1/2 to 3 7/5 pounds. If the chicken is a little larger, you can press down on the breast bone firmly to crack it a little so the chicken flattens out (if your chicken is tied, untying it can help).

TO STORE: Refrigerate chicken in an airtight storage container for up to 3 days.

TO REHEAT: Gently rewarm leftovers in a baking dish in the oven at 350 degrees F or in the microwave.

TO FREEZE: Freeze chicken meat in an airtight freezer-safe storage container for up to 3 months. Let thaw overnight in the refrigerator before reheating.

Air Fryer Turkey Legs

Servings: 3-4
Cooking Time: 30 Minutes

Ingredients:

- 3 Turkey Legs
- 4 tablespoons butter or olive oil
- 1 teaspoon paprika
- ½ teaspoon salt
- ¼ teaspoon garlic powder
- ¼ teaspoon black pepper

Directions:

1. If using butter put it in a small microwave safe bowl melt microwave it until it is melted.
2. Add the seasonings to the melted butter or oil and stir to combine.
3. Pat the legs dry with a paper towel. Brush the seasoning mixture all over the drumsticks. Pull the skin back and brush a little bit underneath.
4. Use parchment paper in the bottom of the air fryer basket if desired to make cleanup easier.
5. Put the legs in the air fryer basket and air fry at 390 for 25-30 minutes.
6. The legs are done when they reach an internal temp of 165 degrees F. Always check the temperature with a meat thermometer, don't just go based on cooking time.
7. If the drumsticks need more cooking time return them to the air fryer for another 5-10 minutes additional time and check the internal temp again.
8. Let them rest for 5-10 minutes before serving.

Notes

Suggested seasoning variations:
Cajun - 1 teaspoon Cajun seasoning, 1/2 teaspoon salt, 1/2 teaspoon black pepper
Old Bay - 1 1/2 teaspoon Old Bay, 1/2 teaspoon garlic powder
Montreal - 2 teaspoons Montreal spicy steak seasoning
Classic - 1 teaspoons poultry seasoning, 1/2 teaspoon salt, 1/2 teaspoon black pepper
Reheat leftover drumsticks in the air fryer at 360 degrees F for about 10 minutes to warm them up.

Air Fryer Grilled Chicken

Servings: 3
Cooking Time: 10 Minutes

Ingredients:

- 3 Boneless Chicken Breasts (I use the perfectly portioned breast)
- 1 teaspoon Garlic powder
- 1 teaspoon Onion powder
- 1/2 teaspoon Paprika powder
- ¼-½ teaspoon Cayenne Powder (depending on spice preference)
- Salt and Pepper to taste

Directions:

1. Preheat your air fryer to 360 degrees.
2. Mix the garlic powder, onion powder, paprika powder, cayenne powder, and salt and pepper. Season the chicken breasts on all sides.
3. Place the chicken breast in the air fryer and cook for 10 minutes, flipping halfway through till it reaches an internal temperature of 165 degrees.
4. These chicken breasts are great on their own, chopped in a salad or wrap.

NOTES
HOW TO REHEAT GRILLED CHICKEN:
Preheat your air fryer to 360 degrees F.
Air fry chicken for 5-8 minutes or until heated through.

Air Fryer Buffalo Chicken Wontons

Servings: 24

Cooking Time: 10 Minutes

Ingredients:
- 2 cups cooked shredded chicken
- 4 ounces cream cheese room temperature
- ⅓ cup buffalo sauce
- ½ cup mozzarella cheese shredded
- ¼ cup green onions sliced
- ½ teaspoon garlic powder
- 24 wonton wrappers
- olive oil spray

Directions:
1. In a medium bowl, stir together the shredded chicken, softened cream cheese buffalo sauce, mozzarella cheese, green onion, and garlic powder.
2. Add a heaping spoonful (about 2 teaspoons) to the center of each wonton. Brush the edges of the wonton wrapper with water and then fold them over to seal. Repeat with the remaining wontons.
3. Spray the air fryer basket generously with olive oil spray and add as many wontons as will fit– make sure not to overcrowd the air fryer.
4. Spray the top of the wontons with olive oil spray and cook at 400F for 8-10 minutes, or until the wontons are golden brown.
5. Serve immediately with ranch or blue cheese dressing.

Notes

These wontons are best enjoyed immediately after they are cooked as they will lose their crispness as they sit.

However, they will keep in the refrigerator for up to 3 days. They can also be frozen and will keep in the freezer for up to 1 month.

Chicken Shawarma Flatbreads

Servings: 4

Cooking Time: 30 Minutes

Ingredients:
- 1 3/4 cup The Pantry Self-Raising Flour
- 1 cup and 3 tablespoons Greek Style Natural Yoghurt
- 300g Chicken Thigh Fillets - diced
- 2 Red Onions
- 4 Garlic Cloves - finely chopped/grated
- Half pack Everyday Essentials Mozzarella
- 1 teaspoon of Cumin
- 1 teaspoon of Smoked Paprika
- 1 teaspoon of Cajun
- 1 teaspoon of Mixed Herbs
- Salt and Pepper
- Oil

Directions:
1. To make the flatbreads, add 1 cup of Greek yoghurt and 1 and 3/4 of self-raising flour to a mixing bowl with a half a teaspoon of salt. Mix with your hands until you have a fluffy dough (it shouldn't stick to your hands so add more flour if it does).
2. Sprinkle some flour onto a worktop, place your dough down and divide into 4 balls. Roll each ball out into a thin, long flatbread shape (make sure it'll fit in your frying pan).
3. Heat up some oil in a pan and add the flatbread. Fry on each side for 3 minutes on a medium heat.
4. Add your chicken thigh fillets to a bowl with 1 tablespoon of Greek yoghurt, 1 teaspoon of smoked paprika, 1 teaspoon of cumin, 1 teaspoon of cajun seasoning and 3 cloves of crushed garlic with some salt and pepper.
5. Place your chicken thighs in the air fryer for 12 minutes on 200 degrees or in the oven in a roasting dish for 35 minutes with a drizzle of oil.
6. Chop up your onion and add that to a frying pan with some oil and cook for 5 minutes.
7. Make up your smoky dressing for the flatbreads by mixing 2 tablespoons of yoghurt, half a teaspoon of paprika, half a teaspoon of cajun and 1 clove of grated

garlic. Spread the dressing over each flatbread.

8. When your chicken is cooked, remove and chop up thinly. Add some chicken and red onion to each flatbread. Tear up your mozzarella and add that too. Finish with some chilli flakes and a garnish of salad if you like.

Lemon Pepper Wings

Servings: 4
Cooking Time: 40 Minutes

Ingredients:

- 1 ½ pounds chicken wings
- 1 tablespoon olive oil
- 2 teaspoons lemon pepper *see note
- 1 ½ teaspoons lemon zest
- 1 clove garlic minced, or half teaspoon garlic powder
- fresh black pepper and kosher salt
- fresh thyme and parsley for garnish optional
- 3 tablespoons melted butter
- 1 teaspoon fresh lemon juice
- For Oven Method Only
- 1 teaspoon baking powder
- 1 tablespoon flour

Directions:

1. Pat chicken wings dry with paper towels.
2. Oven **Directions:**
3. Preheat oven to 425°F.
4. Toss wings with flour and baking powder. Refrigerate at least 15 minutes.
5. Toss wings with olive oil, lemon pepper, lemon zest, and garlic.
6. Line a pan with foil and top with a baking rack. Spray the rack with cooking spray.
7. Bake wings 20 minutes, flip and bake an additional 15 minutes or until crisp. Broil 1 minute each side if desired.
8. Combine butter and lemon juice and toss with wings. Generously season with extra pepper, salt to taste, and fresh thyme if desired. Serve immediately.

Notes

*Some brands of lemon pepper can be excessively salty. Taste your lemon pepper before seasoning the chicken and if it's very salty, reduce the amount.

Flour and baking powder are not required when cooking in an air fryer.

Air Fryer Directions:

Preheat air fryer to 400°F.

Toss wings with olive oil, lemon pepper, lemon zest, and garlic.

Place wings in a single layer in the air fryer basket and cook 10 minutes.

Flip wings and cook an additional 10 minutes or until crispy.

Combine butter and lemon juice and toss with wings. Generously season with extra pepper, salt to taste, and fresh thyme if desired. Serve immediately.

FISH & SEAFOOD RECIPES

Cajun Air Fryer Salmon

Servings: 2
Cooking Time: 10 Minutes

Ingredients:
- cooking spray
- 1 tablespoon Cajun seasoning
- 1 teaspoon brown sugar
- 2 (6 ounce) skin-on salmon fillets

Directions:
1. Gather all ingredients. Preheat the air fryer to 390 degrees F (200 degrees C).
2. Rinse and dry salmon fillets with a paper towel. Mist fillets with cooking spray.
3. Mix together Cajun seasoning and brown sugar in a small bowl until combined; spread onto a plate.
4. Press fillets, flesh-side down, into seasoning mixture.
5. Spray the basket of the air fryer with cooking spray and place salmon fillets skin-side down. Mist salmon again lightly with cooking spray.
6. Close the lid and cook in the preheated air fryer for 8 minutes. Remove from the air fryer and let rest for 2 minutes before serving.

Tips
Increase the cook time by 1 to 2 minutes if you prefer your salmon slightly more done. Do not overcook as it will dry out the salmon.

Air Fryer Cajun Shrimp Dinner

Servings: 4
Cooking Time: 20 Minutes

Ingredients:
- 1 tablespoon Cajun or Creole seasoning
- 24 (1 pound) cleaned and peeled extra jumbo shrimp
- 6 ounces fully cooked Turkey/Chicken Andouille sausage or kielbasa* (sliced)
- 1 medium zucchini (8 ounces, sliced into 1/4-inch thick half moons)
- 1 medium yellow squash (8 ounces, sliced into 1/4-inch thick half moons)
- 1 large red bell pepper (seeded and cut into thin 1-inch pieces)
- 1/4 teaspoon kosher salt
- 2 tablespoons olive oil

Directions:
1. In a large bowl, combine the Cajun seasoning and shrimp, toss to coat.
2. Add the sausage, zucchini, squash, bell peppers, and salt and toss with the oil.
3. Preheat the air fryer 400F.
4. In 2 batches (for smaller baskets), transfer the shrimp and vegetables to the air fryer basket and cook 8 minutes, shaking the basket 2 to 3 times.
5. Set aside, repeat with remaining shrimp and veggies.
6. Once both batches are cooked, return the first batch to the air fryer and cook 1 minute.

Notes
Tip: Buy shrimp still frozen and defrost as needed. Most shrimp arrives at stores frozen so you may as well buy it frozen and defrost it as needed so it as fresh as possible. To defrost shrimp, thaw overnight in the refrigerator.
*check labels for whole30 and gluten-free.

Air Fryer Coconut Shrimp

Servings: 4
Cooking Time: 12 Minutes

Ingredients:
- 1 pound shrimp raw, large, peeled and deveined with tails attached
- ¼ cup all-purpose flour
- ½ teaspoon garlic powder
- ½ teaspoon salt
- ¼ teaspoon black pepper
- 2 large eggs
- ¾ cup unsweetened shredded coconut
- ¼ cup panko breadcrumbs
- Cooking spray

- Sweet chili sauce for serving

Directions:
1. Preheat the air fryer to 360°F. When heated, spray the basket with cooking spray.
2. Combine the flour, garlic powder, salt and pepper in one shallow bowl. Whisk the eggs in a second shallow bowl. Then combine the shredded coconut and panko breadcrumbs in a third shallow bowl.
3. Dip the shrimp into the flour mixture, shaking off any excess. Then dredge the shrimp into the eggs, and finally into the coconut panko mixture, gently pressing to adhere.
4. Place the coconut shrimp in the air fryer so they are not touching, and spray the top of the shrimp. Cook for 10-12 minutes, flipping halfway through.
5. Garnish with chopped parsley, and serve immediately with sweet chili sauce, if desired.

Notes

Storage: Store any leftovers in an airtight container. They will last up to 3 days in the fridge. Reheat in the microwave, in a skillet with a little olive oil, or in an air fryer before serving.

Freezing Instructions: You can freeze the coconut shrimp for up to 3 months. Cool them completely then store them in an airtight bag after. To re-heat, thaw in the fridge overnight and bake in a 350°F oven until heated through.

Substitutes: For best results, follow the recipe as is. However here are some common substitutes that would work well in this recipe.

Instead of the eggs, you can use flax eggs. Replace each egg with 1 tablespoon ground flaxseed + 3 tablespoons water. Let the mixture sit for 10 minutes before dredging the shrimp in it. You can also use low-fat buttermilk.

Instead of all-purpose flour, you can use almond flour or coconut flour.

If you prefer not to use breadcrumbs, you can just use the shredded coconut, although they will not be as crispy on the outside.

Coconut Prawns

Ingredients:
- 15 King prawns
- 1/2 Cup flour
- 2 Tsp salt flakes
- 1 Tsp black pepper
- 1 Tsp garlic powder
- 2 Eggs
- 1/4 Cup coconut
- 1/4 Cup breadcrumbs

Directions:
1. Prepare the prawns by removing the heads, then using kitchen shears, cut the shell down lengthwise to the tail. Remove the shell and legs, leaving the tail. Now use a sharp knife to cut along the centre of the back and remove the vein. Rinse under cold water and pat dry.
2. Place flour, salt, pepper and garlic powder into a bowl. Place the egg into a second bowl and whisk, then place the coconut breadcrumb mixture. Place into the air fryer basket in a single layer and cook for 10 minutes at 200C.
3. Serve with dipping sauce of choice.

Air Fryer Bacon Wrapped Scallops

Servings: 4-6
Cooking Time: 12 Minutes

Ingredients:
- 1 pound large sea scallops
- 1 pound center cut slices of bacon
- 3 tablespoons melted butter
- 1/2 teaspoon of old bay seasoning
- salt and pepper to taste
- 1 teaspoon honey
- 1/4 teaspoonred pepper flakes, optional

Directions:
1. Brush your bacon strips with honey. This will help them carmelize in the air fryer and add a slightly sweet flavor.
2. Place your bacon in your air fryer basket. Cook it at 350 degrees for 5-7 minutes. Toss the bacon slices a few times to keep them

moving. You will slightly precook it so when you wrap it around your scallop it will fully cook since it takes longer for the bacon than the scallop to cook. It is okay to overlap your bacon. You are not looking to get it crisp at this point, just slightly cooked.

3. Pat your scallops with a paper towel and season with salt and pepper.
4. Wrap your scallops with ½-1 slice of bacon. I was able to wrap most of my scallops with a whole slice of bacon but may have to trim the bottom of the bacon depending on how the scallop is shaped.
5. Hold the bacon in place with a toothpick.
6. Melt your butter and incorporate the old bay seasoning. Brush the butter mixture over your scallops.
7. Cook your scallops at 350 for 11-13 minutes. You do not want to overcook your scallops. The bacon should be crispy and the scallops should be firm but slightly bounce back when you touch it. Optional: sprinkle red pepper flakes over top of them.

Air Fryer Frozen Fish Fillets

Servings: 4
Cooking Time: 12 Minutes

Ingredients:
- 4 fish fillets frozen

Directions:
1. Preheat the Air Fryer to 380 degrees Fahrenheit/193 degrees Celcius.
2. If needed, prepare the air fryer basket with olive oil, aluminum foil, parchment paper, or a non stick cooking spray.
3. Place the frozen fish fillets into the air fryer basket in a single layer directly from the freezer. No thawing is needed.
4. Air Fry the fish fillets for 10 minutes.
5. Carefully flip the fish fillets and cook for an additional 2-4 minutes, depending on crispness, and until they are golden brown.

NOTES
Not all air fryers cook the same, this recipe was made with a 5.8qt Cosori air fryer. If you're using a different brand of air fryer, you may need to adjust your cooking time slightly to fit your air fryer.

I love to serve my fish fillets with a side of fries, and hushpuppies, and then garnish with lemon wedges. You can also serve with your favorite sauce, such as tarter sauce.

Lemon-garlic Air Fryer Salmon

Servings: 2
Cooking Time: 10 Minutes

Ingredients:
- 1 tablespoon melted butter
- ½ teaspoon minced garlic
- 2 (6 ounce) fillets center-cut salmon fillets with skin
- ¼ teaspoon lemon-pepper seasoning
- ⅛ teaspoon dried parsley
- cooking spray
- 3 thin slices lemon, cut in half

Directions:
1. Preheat the air fryer to 390 degrees F (200 degrees C).
2. Combine melted butter and minced garlic in a small bowl.
3. Rinse salmon fillets and dry with a paper towel. Brush with butter mixture and sprinkle with lemon-pepper seasoning and parsley.
4. Spray the basket of the air fryer with cooking spray. Place salmon fillets in the basket, skin-side down, and top each with 3 lemon halves.
5. Cook in the preheated air fryer for 8 to 10 minutes. Remove from the air fryer and let rest for 2 minutes before serving.

Air Fryer Fish

Servings: 4

Cooking Time: 25-55 Minutes

Ingredients:
- FOR THE FISH AND FRENCH FRIES:
- Cooking spray
- 1 pound frozen steak fries
- 1 1/2 cups panko breadcrumbs
- 1 1/2 teaspoons kosher salt, divided
- 1/3 cup all-purpose flour
- 1/4 teaspoon freshly ground black pepper
- 2 large eggs
- 2 tablespoons water
- 4 (6-ounce) skinless cod fillets
- Malt vinegar and lemon wedges, for serving
- FOR THE TARTAR SAUCE:
- 1/2 cup mayonnaise
- 1 teaspoon sweet pickle relish
- 1/2 teaspoon Dijon mustard
- 1/2 teaspoon freshly squeezed lemon juice

Directions:
1. MAKE FISH AND FRENCH FRIES:
2. Heat air fryer to 400°F for 10 minutes. Coat the air fryer basket with cooking spray. Working in batches if needed, place 1 pound frozen steak fries in a single layer in the air fryer basket. Air fry for 6 minutes. Flip the fries and air fry until crispy, 6 to 8 minutes more. (Final cook time will depend on your air fryer's capacity and the thickness of your fries.)
3. Meanwhile, place 1 1/2 cups panko breadcrumbs and 1 teaspoon of the kosher salt in a shallow dish and stir to combine. Place 1/3 cup all-purpose flour, the remaining 1/2 teaspoon kosher salt, and 1/4 teaspoon black pepper in a second shallow dish and stir to combine. In a third shallow dish, lightly whisk together 2 large eggs and 2 tablespoons water.
4. When the fries are ready, transfer to a serving bowl and season with kosher salt. Tent the bowl loosely with aluminum foil to keep warm. Reduce the air fryer temperature to 375°F.
5. Halve 4 cod fillets lengthwise into 2 long strips. (There will be a total of 8 pieces.) Working with one stirp at a time, dredge in the flour mixture and shake off the excess. Dip in the egg mixture and let any excess drip off. Dredge in the panko mixture, pressing it in to adhere. Place on a baking sheet or plate.
6. Working in batches if needed, place the fish in a single layer in the air fryer basket. Air fry until golden and crispy, flipping halfway through, about 12 minutes total. The thicker parts of the cod fillet will take longer to cook than the thinner parts toward the tail of the fish, so you may need to cook thicker pieces longer. Meanwhile, make the tartar sauce.
7. MAKE THE TARTAR SAUCE:
8. Place 1/2 cup mayonnaise, 1 teaspoon relish, 1/2 teaspoon Dijon mustard, and 1/2 teaspoon lemon juice in a small bowl and whisk to combine.
9. To serve, place 2 pieces of fish and some steak fries on a plate or arrange inside a newspaper cone. Serve with lemon wedges, malt vinegar, and the tartar sauce.

RECIPE NOTES

Storage: Leftover fish and chips can be refrigerated in an airtight container for up to 2 days. They can be reheated and re-crisped in the air fryer. Heat the air fryer to 350°F for 10 minutes then reheat fish until warmed through, about 5 minutes.

Air Fryer Salmon

Servings: 4

Cooking Time: 10 Minutes

Ingredients:
- 1 pound salmon
- salt and pepper
- 2 tablespoons brown sugar
- 1 teaspoon chili powder
- 1/2 teaspoon paprika
- 1 teaspoon Italian seasoning
- 1 teaspoon garlic powder

Directions:

1. Salt and pepper the salmon. In a small bowl add the brown sugar, chili powder, paprika, Italian seasoning and garlic powder. Rub on the salmon.

2. In the basket of your air fryer add the salmon skin side down. Turn the air fryer to 400 degrees and cook for 10 minutes. If adding asparagus add to the basket after 5 minutes.

Striped Bass With Radish Salsa Verde

Servings: 4

Ingredients:

- 1 clove garlic, pressed
- 1 tbsp. anchovy paste or 3 anchovy fillets, finely chopped
- 1/2 small red onion, finely chopped
- 1 tbsp. red wine vinegar
- 1/2 c. plus 1 tbsp. olive oil, divided
- 1 bunch radishes, diced, leaves separated and finely chopped
- 1 c. flat-leaf parsley leaves, finely chopped
- 1 tsp. tarragon leaves, finely chopped
- 4 6-oz fillets striped bass
- Kosher salt and pepper

Directions:

1. In medium bowl, combine garlic, anchovy paste, onion and vinegar and let sit 5 minutes.

2. Stir in 1/2 cup oil, then radishes and greens, parsley and tarragon.

3. Heat remaining tablespoon oil in medium skillet on medium. Pat fish dry and season with 1/2 teaspoon each salt and pepper and cook, skin side down, until skin is crisp and golden brown, about 7 minutes. Flip and cook until fish is opaque throughout, 3 to 6 minutes more. Serve topped with radish salsa verde.

AIR FRYING DIRECTIONS:

Heat air fryer to 400°F. Pat fish dry, then brush with remaining 1 tablespoon oil and season with 1/2 teaspoon each salt and pepper. Add to air-fryer basket, skin side down, and air-fry until skin is crispy and fish is opaque throughout, 8 to 10 minutes. Serve topped with radish salsa verde.

Air Fried Popcorn Prawns With Burnt Chilli Mayo

Servings: 4

Cooking Time: 25 Minutes

Ingredients:

- 2 Red Chillies
- 450g Cooked King Prawns
- 100g Flour
- 2 Tbsp Cajun Seasoning
- 2 Eggs
- 250g Golden Breadcrumbs
- 1 Lemon
- Olive Oil
- Salt

Directions:

1. In partnership with Mob.

2. Lightly oil the chillies and chuck it into the air fryer, cook on the highest setting for 6-8 mins until charred and cooked throughout.

3. While the chillies roast in the air fryer, open the prawns and drain any liquid from the pack. Dry the prawns with kitchen paper and set aside.

4. Set up 3 medium-sized bowls. Add the flour to the first along with 2 tbsp Cajun seasoning. Crack the eggs into the next bowl and beat with a pinch of salt and 1 tbsp of water. Add the breadcrumbs to the final bowl and stir in 1 tbsp of olive oil. It will clump up to begin with, keep stirring to distribute the oil evenly.

5. Working in batches, pass the prawns through each of the bowls, an even dusting of seasoned flour then through the egg mix. Let the excess drain away then toss through the breadcrumbs. Set the breaded prawns to one side. Repeat with the remaining prawns.

6. Remove the chillies from the air fryer and scrape on the charred skin. Remove the seeds and chop into a paste. Stir through the mayo with the zest of the lemon and season to taste.
7. Add the breaded prawns to the air fryer and cook on high for 8 mins until golden brown and crispy. Toss with salt and a little extra Cajun seasoning. Serve with the spicy mayo and cut the lemon into wedges for squeezing.

Air Fryer Shrimp Tacos

Servings: 6
Cooking Time: 5 Minutes

Ingredients:

- 1 lb shrimp peeled and deveined
- 1 tbsp olive oil
- 1 tsp garlic powder
- 1 tsp paprika
- 1 tsp chili powder
- ½ tsp kosher salt
- ½ tsp cumin
- 6 small tortillas flour or corn
- Cream Sauce
- ½ cup mayonnaise
- ¼ cup sriracha sauce
- 1 tsp fresh lime juice
- Optional toppings
- 1 cup cabbage purple, shredded
- 1 avocado medium, sliced
- 1 cup cotija cheese crumbled
- cilantro garnish

Directions:

1. In a medium bowl, toss shrimp with the olive oil to coat.
2. In a small bowl, stir together the seasonings, then add to the bowl with shrimp. Lightly toss shrimp with seasonings until well coated.
3. Place shrimp in the air fryer basket and air fry at 400 degrees F for 5-7 minutes, until shrimp is cooked.
4. While the shrimp is in the air fryer, in a small bowl, stir together the mayo and hot sauce. Cover and set aside until tacos are assembled.
5. Once the shrimp is done fill tortillas with shrimp, then add additional desired toppings. Drizzle spicy sriracha sauce over tacos before serving.

NOTES
Top Tips
One of the easiest ways to make this simple shrimp taco recipe unique is to have a different taco topping bar every time! All new toppings give all new taste and flavor.
If you want to go simple, you can use some low sodium taco seasoning to create perfect shrimp. You can find it at your local grocery store, and it's a great way to season food fast.
Make this a low carb recipe by skipping the tortillas and just add to lettuce leaves instead. You'll still have that yummy flavor but without the overload of carbs.

Honey Glazed Air Fryer Salmon

Servings: 4
Cooking Time: 8 Minutes

Ingredients:

- 4 Salmon Fillets , skin on (see note 1)
- Salt (see note 2)
- Black Pepper (see note 3)
- 2 teaspoons Soy Sauce (see note 4)
- 1 tablespoon Honey
- 1 teaspoon Sesame Seeds

Directions:

1. Preheat the air fryer (mine takes 2 minutes).
2. Meanwhile: Season each salmon fillet with salt and pepper. Brush the soy sauce into the fish.
3. Place the fillets into the air fryer basket (skin side down) and cook them at 375°F (190°C) for 8 minutes or until ready.
4. About a minute or two before the time is up, glaze each fillet with honey and sprinkle with sesame seeds. Put them back in and finish cooking.
5. Serve with a side of your choice.
Notes

I used 2 large fresh salmon fillets that weighed 1 pound in total. I cut each of them in half to get 4 portions. If you serve filling side dishes like potatoes and salad, one fish fillet per person should be plenty.

Salt – use as much/little as you like. If using normal soy sauce, you might need less salt. If using low sodium, add more salt.

Black pepper – season the fillets to your liking. I like to season them well with pepper. You can use either freshly cracked or ground pepper.

Soy sauce – use either regular one or low sodium. Check recipe note 2.

I used fresh salmon fillets. If possible, choose wild salmon over farmed.

Please note that the cooking time may vary. This will depend on the thickness of the fillets you use and also on the air-fryer brand. Always check the fish for doneness after the time is up. If not ready, pop it in for longer. FDA recommends cooking fish to 145°F (63°C), however, many people like it cooked to medium – 125°F (52°C). I prefer to be safe than sorry, so I follow the FDA recommendation.

Measuring: tsp = teaspoon, tbsp = tablespoon.

Cooking: F = Fahrenheit, C = Celsius.

Bacon-wrapped Shrimp In Air Fryer

Servings: 3-4
Cooking Time: 10 Minutes

Ingredients:
- 1 pound bacon, thinly sliced
- 1 pound raw jumbo shrimp, peeled and deveined
- ½ cup maple syrup
- 4 tablespoons low sodium soy sauce
- 1 teaspoon garlic powder
- ¼ teaspoon red pepper flakes
- Salt and pepper to taste
- Optional: garnish with green onion

Directions:
1. Cut your bacon slices in half, lengthwise. Wrap one slice of your bacon around your shrimp; start at the tail and overlap the first piece of bacon to help hold it on and then wrap up and around the shrimp with as little overlap as possible till you get to the top of the shrimp. Then lay the wrapped shrimp on a baking sheet.
2. Combine the maple syrup, soy sauce, garlic powder, red pepper flakes, salt, and pepper in a small bowl. Use a basting brush to brush the shrimp with the glaze. Flip the shrimp and coat the other side.
3. Preheat the air fryer to 400 degrees F. Place the shrimp in the air fryer, leaving space around them. Cook for 4 minutes and then flip them. Brush them with more sauce and then continue cooking for about 6 minutes more, or until the bacon is crispy.
4. Serve hot and enjoy.

NOTES
HOW TO REHEAT BACON-WRAPPED SHRIMP IN THE AIR FRYER
Preheat the air fryer to 370 degrees F.
Lay the bacon-wrapped shrimp in the air fryer in a single layer.
Cook for 2 to 3 minutes until heated through.

Air Fryer Salmon And Brussels Sprouts

Servings: 4
Cooking Time: 11 Minutes

Ingredients:
- 4 cloves garlic
- 1 teaspoon chopped fresh thyme leaves
- 1 medium lemon
- 2 tablespoons olive oil, divided
- 2 teaspoons kosher salt, divided
- 1 teaspoon freshly ground black pepper, divided
- 4 (7 to 8-ounce) salmon fillets
- Cooking spray
- 1 pound Brussels sprouts
- 1 tablespoon balsamic vinegar
- 1 tablespoon honey

Directions:
1. Mince 4 garlic cloves. Place half in a large bowl and reserve for the Brussels sprouts.

Place the remaining garlic in a small bowl. Chop 1 teaspoon fresh thyme leaves, and juice 1 lemon, and add to the small bowl. Add 1 tablespoon of the olive oil, 1 teaspoon of the kosher salt, and 1/2 teaspoon of the black pepper, and whisk to combine. Brush all over the salmon fillets.

2. Preheat an Instant Vortex Plus 7-in-1 Air Fryer Oven to 400°F and set for 10 minutes. Grease the air fryer racks with cooking spray. Place the salmon fillets skin-side down in the bottom rack of the air fryer, leaving space between the fillets.

3. Add the remaining 1 tablespoon olive oil, 1 teaspoon kosher salt, and 1/2 teaspoon freshly ground black pepper to the large bowl with garlic, and stir to combine. Trim and halve 1 pound Brussels sprouts, add to the bowl, and toss to combine. Place in the top rack of the air fryer above the salmon. Air fry until the salmon is cooked to desired doneness, 6 to 8 minutes.

4. Remove the tray of salmon. Continue air frying the Brussels sprouts until golden brown and crispy, 1 to 3 minutes more. Meanwhile, whisk 1 tablespoon balsamic vinegar and 1 tablespoon honey together until combined.

5. Drizzle the honey vinegar over the finished Brussels sprouts before serving.

RECIPE NOTES

Storage: Leftovers can be refrigerated in an airtight container for up to 2 days.

This recipe was tested in the Instant Vortex Plus 7-in-1 Air Fryer Oven. It will work with any air fryer, but timing may differ slightly.

Air Fryer Chili-lime Cod

Servings: 2

Cooking Time: 10 Minutes

Ingredients:

- 1 teaspoon Paprika
- 1 teaspoon Dried Parsley
- ½ teaspoon Dried Oregano
- ½ teaspoon Chili Powder
- ½ teaspoon Garlic Powder
- ¼ teaspoon Ground Cumin
- ¼ teaspoon Freshly Ground Black Pepper
- 1/8 teaspoon Cayenne Pepper
- 1 Tablespoon Oil
- 2 Cod Fillets about ½ pound each
- Zest of 1 Lime

Directions:

1. In a small bowl combine all of the spices and mix well. Brush the cod filets with 1 tablespoon of oil. Rub the fillets with the spice mixture, coating them well. Refrigerate the spice rubbed cod filets for at least 30 minutes, or up to 12 hours.

2. Preheat the air fryer to 380° F.

3. Place a piece of parchment paper in the bottom of the air fryer basket. Place fillets in the basket in a single layer on top of the parchment paper. You may need to cook the cod in two batches depending on the size of your air fryer.

4. Cook the cod in the air fryer at 380° F for 8-13 minutes. The internal temperature should reach 145° F, and the fish will flake easily and be opaque throughout when it's cooked through.

5. Carefully remove the cooked cod from the air fryer using the parchment paper to help you, and sprinkle the fish with lime zest.

6. Break the fish into large chunks and serve with your favorite toppings in toasted tortillas for delicious fish tacos.

Notes

Grab your tortillas, toast them up, and fill with Air Fryer Chili-Lime Cod and your favorite fish taco toppings

Air Fryer Coconut-fried Shrimp With Dipping Sauce

Servings: 4
Cooking Time: 20 Minutes

Ingredients:
- Coconut-Fried Shrimp
- ½ cup all-purpose flour
- 1 teaspoon salt
- ½ teaspoon baking powder
- ⅔ cup water
- 2 cups shredded sweetened coconut
- ½ cup breadcrumbs
- 1 pound medium or large shrimp, peeled and deveined
- oil, for spraying
- Dipping Sauce
- ½ teaspoon crushed red pepper flakes
- 4 teaspoons rice wine vinegar
- ½ cup orange marmalade

Directions:
1. Coconut-Fried Shrimp
2. In a large bowl, whisk together, flour, salt, and baking powder. Add water and whisk until smooth. Let batter stand for 15 minutes. In a shallow bowl, toss together coconut and breadcrumbs. Place shrimp in batter and coat well. Remove shrimp, one at a time, and press into coconut mixture. Coat well.
3. Spray shrimp on all sides with oil and place in air fryer basket in a single layer. Set temperature to 400 degrees, and air fry for 5 minutes. Turn shrimp, spray with oil, and air fry for 5 minutes more. Repeat with remaining shrimp.
4. Dipping Sauce
5. For the dipping sauce, in a medium saucepan, combine red pepper flakes, vinegar, and marmalade and simmer on low heat for 10 minutes, stirring occasionally.

Frozen Salmon In The Air Fryer

Servings: 2
Cooking Time: 15 Minutes

Ingredients:
- 2 6-oz frozen skinless salmon fillets
- 2 teaspoons olive oil
- 1 teaspoon lemon juice
- 1 teaspoon Dijon mustard
- ½ teaspoon kosher salt
- ½ teaspoon garlic powder
- ¼ teaspoon black pepper
- ⅛-¼ teaspoon cayenne pepper
- Lemon wedges, for serving

Directions:
1. Preheat the air fryer to 390 degrees F.
2. In a small bowl, whisk together the olive oil, lemon juice, Dijon, salt, garlic powder, pepper, and cayenne. Brush the mixture on the top of each fillet.*
3. Place the frozen fillets in a single layer inside and cook for 12 to 18 minutes, depending on thickness, until it reaches an internal temperature of 145 degrees F. Serve with lemon wedges if desired.
4. NOTES
5. *Alternatively, you can cook the salmon without the seasoning for 6 minutes, then brush it onto the defrosted fillets and continue to cook for 6-12 minutes until cooked through.

Crunchy Salmon Circle Cat Treats

Servings: 50
Cooking Time: 4 Hr

Ingredients:
- 1 can boneless, skinless salmon, packed in water (5 ounces)
- ¼ cup water or as needed
- 1 cup oat bran flour or oat flour
- Items Needed
- Food processor
- Parchment paper
- Round cookie cutter (1-inch diameter)

Directions:

1. Drain the canned salmon and place into a food processor. Add the water and blend until the salmon forms a thick paste. If the mixture is too thick, add water, one tablespoon at a time, until the salmon is puréed.
2. Add the salmon paste to a bowl and add the flour. Mix well until you can form a ball with the dough.
3. Place the dough onto a clean work surface lined with parchment paper and roll out to ¼-inch-thick.
4. Cut out the dough into 1-inch circles using a round cookie cutter.
5. Place the dough circles evenly between the Food Dehydrator trays.
6. Set temperature to 145°F and time to 4 hours, then press Start/Stop.
7. Remove the treats when done and crispy and crunchy. Cool completely, then serve to your pet.

Air Fryer Spanish Garlic Prawns

Servings: 2
Cooking Time: 15 Minutes

Ingredients:
- 1 bag of The Fishmonger Garlic & Herb Raw King Prawns
- 6-8 cloves of Nature's Pick Garlic
- 1 handful of Nature's Pick Cut Parsley
- 2 tablespoons of The Pantry Lemon Juice
- 2 x Village Bakery Bake At Home White Rolls
- 200g Butter
- 1 teaspoon of Chilli Flakes
- 1 tablespoon of Smoked Paprika
- SHOP THE INGREDIENTS

Directions:
1. Place the garlic and herb prawns in a bowl with 1 tablespoon of smoked paprika, 1 teaspoon of flour and salt and pepper. Drizzle with oil and place them in the air fryer on 200 degrees for 7 minutes until crispy. Alternatively, if you don't have an air fryer, don't add flour or oil and set aside whilst you make the garlic butter sauce.
2. Whilst they are cooking, make the garlic sauce. Finely chop 6 cloves of garlic. Place 100g of butter in a pan and add garlic in (leave a teaspoon of garlic for the garlic butter on the side), cook until butter has melted.
3. Add in one teaspoon of chilli flakes and two tablespoons of lemon juice.
4. Once prawns are cooked, add them into the garlic butter sauce or if you're not using an air fryer, add them into the butter to cook for 7 minutes. Chop up a handful of parsley and add that in then put into small dishes.
5. To make the garlic butter, add 100g of butter into a bowl and add half a teaspoon of chilli flakes, a tablespoon of the prawns sauce, half a teaspoon of chopped parsley and a teaspoon of chopped garlic. (If you are cooking the garlic butter jacket potatoes too, make double the amount).
6. Serve the prawns with warm bread and the garlic butter on the side.

Air Fryer Scallops

Servings: 4
Cooking Time: 5 Minutes

Ingredients:
- 1/2 cup Italian breadcrumbs
- 1/2 teaspoon garlic powder
- 1/4 teaspoon salt
- 1/2 teaspoon black pepper
- 2 tablespoons butter, melted
- 1 pound sea scallops, patted dry

Directions:
1. Preheat your air fryer to 390 degrees F.
2. In a shallow bowl, mix the breadcrumbs, garlic powder, salt, and pepper together. Pour melted butter into a second shallow bowl.
3. Dredge each scallop through the melted butter, then roll in the breadcrumb mixture until they're completely coated; set aside on a plate.

4. Lightly spray the preheated air fryer basket with cooking spray. Arrange scallops in a single layer, working in batches if necessary.
5. Air fry the scallops for 2 minutes. Use tongs to carefully flip them over, then air fry for 3 more minutes until opaque and golden brown.

NOTES
How to Reheat Scallops in the Air Fryer:
Preheat your air fryer to 390 degrees.
Cook leftover sea scallops in the air fryer for 2 to 3 minutes, until warmed thoroughly.
HOW TO COOK FROZEN SCALLOPS IN THE AIR FRYER:
Preheat your air fryer to 390 degrees.
Place frozen scallops in the air fryer and cook for about 7 minutes, flipping them halfway through.

Air Fryer Mexican Shrimp

Servings: 4
Cooking Time: 10 Minutes

Ingredients:
- 1 lb. white shrimp, peeled, deveined, and tails removed
- 1 tablespoon olive oil
- 1 teaspoon ground cumin
- 1 teaspoon chili powder (optional for a kick)
- 1/2 teaspoon paprika
- 1/2 teaspoon garlic powder
- 1/2 teaspoon dried oregano (or Italian seasoning)
- 1/2 teaspoon salt
- 1/4 teaspoon ground black pepper
- 1 tablespoon fresh cilantro, chopped (optional, for garnish)

Directions:
1. In a medium bowl, add shrimp, olive oil, cumin, chili powder, paprika, garlic powder, oregano, salt and pepper. Toss well to coat and set aside to marinate for 15 minutes (if you have the time).
2. Transfer the shrimp into the air fryer basket. Cook at 350 F for 8-10 minutes, shaking the basket once halfway through.
3. Sprinkle with cilantro on top and serve.

4. NOTES
5. How to store: Leftover shrimp will keep in the refrigerator for up to 3-4 days when stored in an airtight container. Allow it to cool to room temperature before placing in the refrigerator.
6. How to reheat shrimp: Reheat in a skillet over medium-low heat until warmed through, about 5 minutes, or in the microwave for about 1 minute. You can also reheat in a preheated oven or air fryer at 300F for about 5 minutes until warmed through. Reheating can cause the shrimp to be a little drier than when served fresh. You can also eat leftovers cold on a salad.
7. Alternate cooking methods: You can cook this shrimp in the oven by spreading it evenly on a parchment-lined quarter sheet baking pan and baking in a 400 F preheated oven for 8-10 minutes until the shrimp turns pink. You can also cook over the stovetop by sautéing over medium-high heat for 5 minutes until shrimp turns pink and nicely browned.

Air Fryer Frozen Shrimp

Servings: 3
Cooking Time: 10 Minutes

Ingredients:
- 1 pound (454 g) frozen raw shrimp
- oil spray or vegetable oil , to coat shrimp
- salt , to taste
- black pepper , to taste
- EQUIPMENT
- Air Fryer

Directions:
1. Evenly coat the frozen shrimp with oil spray or vegetable oil. Season with salt & pepper (you do not need to thaw the shrimp).
2. Place the frozen shrimp in the air fryer basket and spread in an even layer (make sure they aren't overlapping).
3. Air Fry at 400°F/205°C for 8-14 minutes (depending on the size of your shrimp and your air fryer), flipping the shrimp halfway

through cooking. Check for doneness & air fry longer if needed.

NOTES

Air Frying Tips and Notes:

Cook Frozen - Do not thaw first.

Shake or turn if needed. Don't overcrowd the air fryer basket.

If cooking in multiple batches, the first batch will take longer to cook if Air Fryer is not already pre-heated. Recipe timing is based on a non-preheated air fryer.

Recipes were tested in 3.4 to 6 qt air fryers. If using a larger air fryer, the recipe might cook quicker so adjust cooking time.

Remember to set a timer to shake/flip/toss as directed in recipe.

Air Fryer Salmon With Skin

Servings: 3

Cooking Time: 7 Minutes

Ingredients:

- 3 Salmon fillets
- 1 Tablespoon Olive oil substitute with any other flavourless oil of choice
- 1 teaspoon smoked paprika substitute with sweet paprika
- 1 teaspoon garlic granules substitute with freshly minced garlic cloves
- 1/2 teaspoon onion granules
- salt and freshly ground black pepper to taste I used less than a teaspoon each
- Lemon wedge to serve

Directions:

1. Preheat the air fryer at 200C/400F for 5 minutes
2. To a small bowl, add smoked paprika, garlic granules, onions granules, salt and black pepper and stir to combine.
3. Pat the salmon dry with a kitchen papper towel. Drizzle the olive oil on the fillets.
4. Sprinkle the fish seasoning on each of the fillets and pat it down into the fish using your hands.
5. Carefully place the salmon in the air fryer basket and cook at 200C/400F for 7 to 8 minutes or until the internal temperature

registers 120F/50C. The fish would continue to cook as it rests. You will tknow the fish is done if it flakes apart easily with a fork.

6. Remove it from the air fryer and serve with other sides of choice

NOTES

How to store

Fridge: leave the salmon to cool completely and store in the fridge for up to 3 days in an airtight container.

Freezer: You can freeze the salmon for up to 3 months in an airtight container or a Ziploc freezer bag making sure you take out as much air as possible.

Blackened Air Fryer Salmon Bites

Servings: 4

Cooking Time: 7 Minutes

Ingredients:

- 4 6 ounce skinless salmon filets (diced in 1 inch chunks)
- olive oil spray
- 1 tablespoon sweet paprika
- 1/2 teaspoon dried cayenne pepper
- 1 teaspoon garlic powder
- 1 teaspoon dried thyme
- 1 teaspoon dried oregano
- 1 teaspoon kosher salt
- 1/8 teaspoon black pepper
- lemon wedges (for serving)
- chopped parsley (for garnish)
- brown rice (optional for serving)

Directions:

1. Place salmon in a large bowl and spritz the salmon with oil.
2. Combine all the spices, from paprika to black pepper in a small bowl and mix. Rub all over the salmon.
3. Spray the basket with oil.
4. Place salmon in the air fryer basket and air fry 400F about 5 to 7 minutes, shaking halfway until the salmon is cooked through in the center and browned all over.
5. Serve with lemon wedges and fresh parsley.

Air-fryer Salmon Cakes

Servings: 2

Ingredients:

- Cooking spray
- 2 (7.5 ounce) cans unsalted pink salmon (with skin and bones)
- 1 large egg
- ½ cup whole-wheat panko breadcrumbs
- 2 tablespoons chopped fresh dill
- 2 tablespoons canola mayonnaise
- 2 teaspoons Dijon mustard
- ¼ teaspoon ground pepper
- 2 lemon wedges

Directions:

1. Coat the basket of an air fryer with cooking spray.
2. Drain salmon; remove and discard any large bones and skin. Place the salmon in a medium bowl. Add egg, panko, dill, mayonnaise, mustard and pepper; stir gently until combined. Shape the mixture into four 3-inch-diameter cakes.
3. Coat the cakes with cooking spray; place in the prepared basket. Cook at 400 degrees F until browned and an instant-read thermometer inserted into the thickest portion registers 160 degrees F, about 12 minutes. Serve with lemon wedges.

Harissa Salmon With Crispy Chickpeas

Servings: 2

Ingredients:

- 230 g (2) salmon fillets
- 3 tbsp Harissa paste, Inspired To Cook
- 1 tbsp olive oil
- 400 g chickpeas
- 1/2 tsp black pepper
- 200 g tenderstem broccoli

Directions:

1. Preheat the air fryer to 180, and prepare the salmon by adding 1 tbsp of harissa paste over each fillet and rub it all over the with the back of a spoon

2. Drain the can of chickpeas, and pour them onto a plate, pat dry with kitchen roll, and pour over the oil, pepper and 1 tbsp of the harissa paste, give them a roll around to combine and pick up all the flavours
3. Add the fillets, and what chickpeas you can fit into the air fryer and fry for 10 minutes finish off the rest of the chickpeas and the broccoli .

Air Fryer Fish Sticks

Servings: 3
Cooking Time: 9 Minutes

Ingredients:

- 12 frozen fish sticks

Directions:

1. Preheat your air fryer to 400 degrees.
2. Place frozen fish sticks in the air fryer in one layer not touching.
3. Cook for 9-10 minutes, flipping halfway, until warmed thoroughly.
4. Remove from the air fryer and enjoy!

NOTES
HOW TO REHEAT FISH STICKS IN THE AIR FRYER
Preheat your air fryer to 400 degrees.
Cook leftover fish sticks in the air fryer for 1 to 2 minutes, until fully warmed then enjoy!

Soy & Lemongrass Salmon Fillets

Servings: 2

Ingredients:

- 2 x 150g salmon fillets
- For the marinade
- 2 tbsp light soy sauce
- 1 tsp sesame oil
- 1 tsp light brown sugar
- 1 lemongrass stalk, finely sliced
- 2 garlic cloves, crushed
- 2cm piece ginger, grates
- A pinch black pepper
- A pinch chilli flakes
- Topping

- 1/2 red chilli sliced finely
- A few leaves coriander, sliced finely
- A pinch sesame seeds
- 200g fine green beans
- 200g cherry tomatoes
- 1 tbsp oil
- COOKING MODE
- When entering cooking mode - We will enable your screen to stay 'always on' to avoid any unnecessary interruptions whilst you cook!

Directions:
1. In a shallow dish, mix marinade ingredients together. Add salmon and turn over to coat both sides with marinade. Top with chilli slices, coriander and sesame seeds. Place in a refrigerator and leave to marinade for 1 hour.
2. Meanwhile in a bowl, toss green beans and tomatoes. Insert the crisper plates in both drawers. Add salmon fillets to zone 1 drawer, add beans and tomatoes to zone 2 drawer and insert drawers into unit.
3. Select zone 1, select AIR FRY, set temperature to 200°C and set time to 10 minutes. Select zone 2, select AIR FRY set temperature to 200°C and set time to 8 minutes. Select SYNC. Select START/STOP to begin. When zone 2 drawer reaches 4 minutes, give the drawer a shake.
4. When cooking is complete, transfer salmon and vegetables to a plate and serve with noodles or rice. Garnish with coriander leaves if desired. Serve immediately.

Air Fryer Scallops Recipe
Servings: 2-4
Cooking Time: 4-5 Minutes

Ingredients:
- 1 pound dry sea scallops (12 to 16 medium)
- 1 medium lemon
- 1 clove garlic
- 1 tablespoon fresh dill, plus more for garnish (optional)
- 2 tablespoons olive oil
- 1/2 teaspoon kosher salt
- 1/4 teaspoon freshly ground black pepper

Directions:
1. Gently peel off the side muscle from 1 pound scallops if they are still attached. Pat the scallops dry with paper towels.
2. Finely grate the zest from 1 medium lemon until you have 1 teaspoon zest and set aside for garnish. Juice the lemon until you have 2 tablespoons juice and place in a medium bowl. Mince 1 garlic clove and finely chop 1 tablespoon fresh dill if using (plus more for garnish if desired), and add both to the bowl.
3. Add 2 tablespoons olive oil, 1/2 teaspoon kosher salt, and 1/4 teaspoon black pepper, and stir to combine. Add the scallops and toss gently to coat. Let marinate for 10 minutes at room temperature. Meanwhile, heat an air fryer to 390 to 400°F.
4. Use tongs to transfer the scallops into the air fryer basket in a single layer, leaving the marinade in the bowl. Air fry for 2 minutes. Flip the scallops and air fry until the scallops are firm and the internal temperature is 115°F, about 3 minutes more (they may not be evenly browned).
5. Transfer the scallops to a plate and garnish with the lemon zest and more dill.

RECIPE NOTES
Storage: Scallops are best eaten immediately, but leftovers can be refrigerated in an airtight container up to 2 days.

SANDWICHES & BURGERS RECIPES

Air-fryer Cheeseburger Spring Rolls

Servings: 20
Cooking Time: 30 Minutes

Ingredients:
- 500g Woolworths BBQ classic beef burgers
- 3 gherkins, finely chopped
- 3 tbs tomato sauce (save 1 tbs to serve)
- 2 tbs American mustard (save 1 tbs to serve)
- 1 cup shredded pizza cheese
- 300g frozen spring roll pastry, thawed
- 5ml olive oil cooking spray

Directions:
1. Preheat air fryer to 180°C.
2. Using hands, combine beef burgers, gherkins, sauce, mustard and cheese in a
3. large bowl.
4. Place 1 pastry sheet on bench with 1 corner pointing towards you. Place 1 slightly heaped tablespoonful of mince mixture in middle of pastry. Fold corner nearest to you over filling then roll up, folding in sides to enclose filling. Transfer to a tray and cover with a damp tea towel (see Tip). Repeat with remaining pastry sheets and mince mixture to make a total of 20 spring rolls.
5. Tip: Covering rolls with a damp tea towel prevents them drying out.
6. Spray air-fryer basket with oil. Place half of the spring rolls in basket and spray with oil. Cook for 15 minutes, turning halfway through cooking, or until golden and crisp. Repeat with remaining spring rolls. Serve spring rolls drizzled with extra tomato sauce and mustard.

Air Fryer Turkey Burgers

Servings: 4
Cooking Time: 15 Minutes

Ingredients:
- 1 pound lean ground turkey
- ½ cup dried breadcrumbs
- 1 large egg
- 1 tablespoon ketchup
- ½ tablespoon Worcestershire sauce
- 1 teaspoon seasoning salt
- Black pepper, to taste
- Hamburger buns
- Lettuce, tomato, onion, or your favorite burger toppings

Directions:
1. Place the ground turkey in a mixing bowl with the breadcrumbs, egg, ketchup, Worcestershire sauce, seasoning salt, and pepper.
2. Use a fork to mix the contents of the bowl together well, being sure not to overmix.
3. Shape into four ½-inch thick round patties and place them on a large plate. Chill the patties in the fridge for at least 30 minutes
4. Preheat an air fryer to 360 degrees F for 5 minutes. Spray the air fryer basket with cooking spray, then place the burgers in an even layer in the basket.
5. Air fry for 15 minutes, flipping halfway through until an internal temperature of 165 degrees F is reached.

Air Fryer Hamburgers

Servings: 4
Cooking Time: 10 Minutes

Ingredients:
- 1 ½ pounds lean ground beef
- 1 tablespoon Worcestershire sauce
- salt & pepper to taste
- ¼ cup barbecue sauce optional
- for serving
- 4 hamburger buns
- lettuce, tomatoes, pickles, onions

Directions:
1. Preheat air fryer to 400°F.
2. Combine beef, Worcestershire sauce, and salt and pepper. Gently mix to combine.

3. Divide the mixture into four ½" thick patties and place in the air fryer in a single layer. Use your thumb to place a small indent in the middle of the burger patty.
4. Brush the burgers with the barbecue sauce, if using.
5. Cook 5 minutes, flip burgers, and cook an additional 4-6 minutes or until the burgers reach 160°F.

notes

When mixing burgers, mix gently.

1 tablespoon of grated onion can be added to the beef mixture for extra flavor.

Air fryers can vary, check the burgers early to ensure they don't overcook.

Cheese can be added during the last 1 minute of cooking time.

Keep leftover air fryer burgers in a covered container in the refrigerator for up to 5 days. Freeze them in zippered bags for up to 8 weeks.

Air Fryer Amazing Burgers

Servings: 4
Cooking Time: 12 Minutes

Ingredients:
- 1.25 lb. (567 g) ground beef
- 1 teaspoon (5 ml) garlic powder
- 1 Tablespoon (15 ml) Worcestershire , fish sauce, or soy sauce (fish sauce is our favorite)
- 1/2 teaspoon (2.5 ml) salt , or to taste
- Lots of black pepper
- oil spray , for coating
- BURGER ASSEMBLY:
- 4 Buns , + optional cheese, pickles, lettuce, onion, tomato, avocado, cooked bacon etc.
- EQUIPMENT
- Air Fryer
- Instant Read Thermometer (optional)

Directions:
1. Preheat the Air Fryer at 380°F/193°C for about 4-5 minutes.
2. In bowl, combine beef, garlic, garlic powder Worcestershire sauce (or sauce of choice),

salt and pepper. Mix everything until just combined.
3. Divide and flatten into 4 patties about 4" wide (don't pack the patties too firmly or else you'll have a dense burger - form just enough so that the patty holds its shape). Spray both sides with oil and spray the air fryer basket. If you have a smaller air fryer, you'll might need to cook in two batches.
4. Air Fry at 380°F/193°C for about 8-12 minutes, flip after 6 minutes. Cook to your preference or until the internal temperature reaches 160°F/71°C. Timing will vary depending on thickness of patties and individual air fryer model.
5. For Cheeseburgers: add the slices of cheese on top of the cooked patties. Air fry at 380°F/193°C for about 30 seconds to 1 minute to melt the cheese.
6. For best juiciness, cover the patties and let rest for about 3 minutes. While patties are resting, warm the buns in the air fryer at 380°F/193°C for about 1 minute. Serve on buns, topped with your favorite burger toppings.

Air Fryer Club Sandwich

Servings: 2
Cooking Time: 20 Minutes

Ingredients:
- 3 slice/s thick sandwich bread (we used Toastie bread)
- 6 rasher/s smoked streaky bacon
- 2 medium vine tomatoes
- 6 tsp Essential Mayonnaise
- 1/2 x 1 iceberg lettuce
- 150g leftover cooked turkey or chicken, thinly sliced
- 4 slice/s Emmental cheese
- salted crisps, to serve (optional)

Directions:
1. Toast the bread until golden brown (you can do this in the air fryer: put the bread on top of the rack and cook at 200°C for 4-6 minutes, turning every minute or so).

Meanwhile, lay the bacon rashers on top of the rack in the basket of the air fryer and air-fry at 200°C for 6-8 minutes, turning them halfway, until very crisp.

2. Slice each tomato into 4-5 slices and season (snack on the ends – chef's treat). Spread each slice of toast with 2 tsp mayonnaise. Tear the iceberg so you have 6-8 pieces about the same size as the bread. Divide the ingredients over 2 slices of toast, layering lettuce, then tomatoes, sliced chicken, bacon and cheese. Put one dressed slice on top of the other and close the sandwich with the empty slice, mayo-side down.

3. Insert 4 toothpicks into the sandwich. Slice with a bread knife into 4 triangles and serve immediately with crisps, if liked.

Cook's tip

If you don't have leftovers to hand, use a rolling pin to flatten 4 medium chicken breasts (150g each) between baking parchment, until they are of even thickness. Season, drizzle with 1 tbsp oil and air-fry at 180°C for 15-18 minutes, until cooked through, the juices run clear and there is no pink meat; you can check with a meat thermometer (75°C). Leave to rest for 10 minutes.

Customer safety tips

Follow manufacturer's instructions and advice for specific foods

Pre-heat the air fryer to the correct temperature

If cooking different foods together, be aware that they may require different times and temperatures

Spread food evenly – do not overcrowd pan/chamber

Turn food midway through cooking

Check food is piping/steaming hot and cooked all the way through

Aim for golden colouring – do not overcook

Turkey Burgers

Servings: 4
Cooking Time: 20 Minutes

Ingredients:

- 450g turkey mince
- 4 x spring onions
- 70ml Greek yoghurt
- 100g fresh breadcrumbs – made from 2 slices village bakery sliced bread
- Sae salt and black pepper
- 1 x pack 4 Burger buns
- Tomato, lettuce, red onion, cucumber and mayonnaise to serve

Directions:

1. Divide the mixture into 4 and roll into balls.
2. Flatten into burger shapes – put into the fridge to set for 10 mins.
3. Pre heat the airfryer to 180°C.
4. Put the burgers onto the fry tray – don't overlap.
5. Close the fry basket and cook for 20 mins.
6. Meanwhile toast the cut sides of the burger buns.
7. Spread some mayo on the bases – then some slices tomato, lettuce leaves, red onion and cucumber.
8. Top with a burger, then the bread top and serve.

Air Fryer Cheeseburger Bombs

Servings: 8
Cooking Time: 5 Minutes

Ingredients:

- 8 ounces crescent roll dough
- 1 1/2 pounds hamburger meat
- 1 1/2 cups cheddar cheese

Directions:

1. Preheat the Air Fryer to 400 degrees Fahrenheit.
2. Create meatballs with hamburger meat and cook at 400 degrees Fahrenheit for 10-12 minutes, depending on your preferred doneness.
3. Allow meatballs to cool for a few minutes after air frying.
4. Lay out each crescent roll sheet. Add cheese to the top of each dough sheet.

5. Top the cheese with a meatball, and then pinch the dough closed and use your hands to round them into little balls.
6. Place the cheeseburger balls into the basket of the air fryer and cook at 350 degrees Fahrenheit for 5 minutes.
7. Carefully remove cheeseburger bombs and dip into your favorite sauces such as mustard, ketchup, or BBQ sauce.

NOTES

This recipe was made with a 1700 watt 5.8 qt Cosori air fryer. All air fryers cook a little differently. You may need to adjust the cooking time based on your specific brand of air fryer.

You can use premade fresh or frozen meatballs to make this dish. Just add a little cooking time to the meatballs if you are making them from frozen.

You can change this recipe in several different ways. Consider seasoning the meatballs with your favorite burger seasoning, or simple things such as onion powder, salt, and pepper.

You can add additional items to the homemade meatballs or just to the burger bombs themselves. Consider adding items such as diced jalapenos, diced onions, or even small pieces of bacon.

Lentil Veggie Burger Recipe

Servings: 6
Cooking Time: 35 Minutes

Ingredients:
- Patties
- 3/4 cup (150 g) dry red lentils
- 1/2 cup (90 g) dry quinoa
- 2 cups (480 ml) vegetable broth
- 3 Tbsp ground chia seeds + 1/4 cup water
- 1/2 cup (60 g) pumpkin seeds (or nuts/seeds of choice)
- 2/3 cup (55 g) quick oats (gluten-free if needed)
- 1 Tbsp tomato paste
- 1 1/2 Tbsp tamari or coconut aminos
- 1 small onion chopped
- 3 garlic cloves chopped
- 2 tsp smoked paprika
- 1 tsp ground cumin
- 3/4 tsp sea salt or less/more to taste
- Black pepper to taste
- Other Ingredients:
- 2 Tbsp oil for frying
- Vegan BBQ sauce optional
- 6 burger buns regular or gluten-free
- Fresh veggies of choice e.g. tomatoes, lettuce, onion, cucumber
- Burger sauce

Directions:
1. You can watch the video in the post for visual instructions.
2. First, add the quinoa, red lentils, and veggie broth to a saucepan and bring it to a boil over high heat. Then, reduce the heat and simmer for about 15 minutes, or until the liquid absorbs. Increase the heat for a minute or two to evaporate all remaining liquid.
3. Meanwhile, mix three tablespoons of ground chia seeds with 1/4 cup of water and set it aside to thicken. If you don't have ground chia seeds, blend the seeds for a few seconds in a blender or coffee/spice grinder.
4. Next, process the oats and pumpkin seeds in a food processor/blender for a few seconds. Then, add all the remaining ingredients to the processor, including the chia mixture, cooked quinoa, and lentils, and pulse again into a slightly chunky burger dough.
5. Be careful not to over-process the mixture into a paste, as the burgers should have some texture. If the mixture is too sticky, add some more oats. If it's too dry, add a little water.
6. Divide and shape the mixture into 6 burger patties with your hands.
7. Heat the oil in a large frying pan/ skillet (for alternative cooking methods, check the FAQs). Once hot, add three burger patties (or how many your pan will fit while not touching and easily able to flip) and cook for around 10 minutes, flipping halfway, until the burgers are firm and lightly crisp.
8. Repeat this with the remaining burgers.
9. Assemble the vegan hamburger with the salad veggies of your choice. Enjoy with a side of wedges and a salad.

Notes

Adjust the size: You can divide the mixture into smaller style 'fritters' or even smaller 'nuggets' with this same quinoa lentil burger mixture.

Cooking time may vary: Especially if you change the size of the patties.

For even-sized burgers: Divide the quinoa lentil mixture by weight (each weighing about 135-140 grams).

Store: Allow the cooked lentil patties to cool, and store any leftovers in an airtight container in the fridge for up to 5 days.

Frozen Hamburgers In The Air Fryer

Servings: 4
Cooking Time: 15 Minutes

Ingredients:
- 4 frozen hamburgers (1/4 to 1/2 pounds each)
- OPTIONAL (FOR SERVING)
- Hamburger buns
- Cheese
- Lettuce
- Tomato

Directions:
1. Preheat your air fryer to 370 degrees.
2. Place the frozen hamburgers in the air fryer and cook for 10 to 20 minutes, depending on cook preference (15 to 17 minutes for medium).
3. (optional) Turn your air fryer off and place a piece of cheese on each burger. Close your air fryer and let the cheese melt with the residual heat.
4. Remove the hamburgers from the air fryer and enjoy!

NOTES
Rare (125 degrees): approximately 13 minutes
Medium Rare (135 degrees): approximately 14 to 16 minutes
Medium (145 degrees): approximately 15 to 17 minutes
Medium Well (155 degrees): approximately 16 to 18 minutes
Well Done (160 degrees): approximately 17 to 20 minutes

Air Fryer Frozen Turkey Burgers

Servings: 4
Cooking Time: 18 Minutes

Ingredients:
- 4 frozen raw turkey patties , usually sold as either 1/4 lb.(113g) or 1/3 lb.(150g)
- salt , to taste if needed
- Lots of black pepper
- oil spray , for coating
- BURGER ASSEMBLY:
- 4 Buns , + optional cheese, pickles, lettuce, onion, tomato, avocado, cooked bacon etc.
- EQUIPMENT
- Air Fryer
- Instant Read Thermometer (optional)

Directions:
1. Spray both sides of frozen turkey patties with oil. Season with optional salt and pepper. Spray the air fryer basket with oil. Place the patties in the basket in a single layer. Cook in batches if needed.
2. 1/4 lb. frozen turkey patties: Air Fry at 380°F/193°C for a total of about 12-17 minutes. After the first 10 minutes flip the patties and continue Air Frying at 380°F/193°C for another 2-7 minutes or until it's cooked to your preferred doneness. The internal temperature should be 165°F/74°C.
3. 1/3 lb. frozen turkey patties: Air Fry at 380°F/193°C for a total of about 13-18 minutes. After the first 10 minutes flip the patties and continue Air Frying at 380°F/193°C for another 3-8 minutes or until it's cooked to your preferred doneness. The internal temperature should be 165°F/74°C.
4. Cheeseburgers: add the slices of cheese on top of the cooked patties. Air fry at 380°F/193°C for about 30 seconds to 1 minute to melt the cheese.
5. Cover the patties and let rest for 3 minutes. Warm the buns in the air fryer at 380°F/193°C for about 3 minutes while patties are resting. Serve on buns, topped with your favorite burger toppings.

Printed in Great Britain
by Amazon